greatcookingclassics

contents

classic food

Food is a lip-smacking way to experience the world, whether your experience comes through travelling the globe or dining at the Thai restaurant just down the road. Food spans borders and unites people in their common appetite for appealing dishes. The cuisines of many regions, with the help of inspired cooks, have been made and shared far from home. Fabulous new tastes inspire the repetition of a recipe, and soon something new transforms into an old, much-requested favourite. A classic dish is born over time – tried, tested and perfected in families, for friends, and in regions, cultures and countries.

Ingredients that can be produced in abundance in a locale become mainstays of the local cuisine. The bounty of seafood pulled from the Mediterranean Sea, for example, is the inspiration for the famous French bouillabaisse, just as the catch from the China Sea has led to the ever-popular salt and pepper squid. The ubiquitous tomato, grown in many temperate regions around the globe, takes its famous place in the cuisines of Italy (think spaghetti bolognese), Spain (gazpacho), France (ratatouille), Lebanon (fattoush), India (dhal) and Thailand (spicy beef salad).

Ingenuity has also played a part in the development of many dishes; wrappers, for example, have taken the form of vine leaves in Greece (dolmades), cabbage leaves in Hungary (cabbage rolls), rice paper in Vietnam (fresh rice paper rolls with prawns), tortillas in Mexico (beef burritos) and lettuce leaves in China (sang choy bow). Cool regions have developed hearty, warming meals such as shepherd's pie (England), osso bucco (Italy) and coq au vin (France), while the hot spots of the globe have produced cooling dishes such as ceviche (Latin America), gado gado (Indonesia) and cucumber and mint raita (India).

Another common desire the world over is for all things sweet. Australia's pavlova will go a long way towards satisfying a sweet tooth but, if you'd prefer, indulge in tarte tatin (France), pumpkin pie (United States of America), tiramisu (Italy), sacher torte (Austria) or delightfully sticky custard tarts (Portugal).

In this magnificent new volume, we've attempted to include the most exciting, yet consistently requested, recipes the world has come up with. We've considered the recipes of all countries on all continents to devise and compile a collection of the greatest dishes on earth. The timeless nature of the recipes contained here ensure that *Great Cooking Classics* will be a book that you turn to regularly, whether you'd like to experiment with a new recipe (that is, nevertheless, a guaranteed success) or to re-create favourites from your travels.

dips & finger food

Starters may differ wildly in form and presentation between one country and another, but there is no better way to set the tone of a meal than with a delicious morsel (or two or three) of finger food.

guacamole MEXICO

PREPARATION TIME **20 MINUTES**

Guacamole is an avocado salad from Mexico; it is sometimes used as an accompaniment but is most commonly eaten as a dip. For extra flavour, try adding either crushed garlic, chopped green onion, finely chopped fresh red chilli or a few drops of Tabasco sauce.

1 medium white onion (150g)
2 small tomatoes (260g), seeded
2 medium avocados (500g)
2 tablespoons lime juice
2 tablespoons finely chopped
 fresh coriander

1 Chop onion and tomatoes finely.

2 Using a fork, mash avocados in medium bowl until almost smooth. Add onion, tomato, juice and coriander; mix well.

makes 2½ cups (600g)

per tablespoon 3.3g fat; 138kJ (33 cal)
serving suggestion Serve guacamole with corn chips as a dipper; it is also good with tacos, nachos and other Mexican dishes.

hummus   MIDDLE-EAST

PREPARATION TIME **10 MINUTES** (plus standing time) COOKING TIME **50 MINUTES**

Hummus is a Middle-Eastern dip made with tahini, a sesame seed paste. You can buy tahini from selected supermarkets and delicatessens. If desired, 450g canned chickpeas, rinsed and drained, may be used instead of dried chickpeas. Hummus can be made three days ahead; store, covered, in the refrigerator.

¾ cup (150g) dried chickpeas
1 teaspoon salt
1 clove garlic, quartered
⅓ cup (90g) tahini
¼ cup (60ml) lemon juice
pinch cayenne pepper
1 tablespoon finely chopped
    fresh flat-leaf parsley
2 teaspoons extra virgin olive oil

1 Place chickpeas in medium bowl, cover with cold water; stand overnight.

2 Drain chickpeas, place in medium saucepan, cover with fresh water. Bring to a boil; simmer, covered, about 50 minutes or until chickpeas are tender. Drain chickpeas over large heatproof bowl. Reserve ⅓ cup (80ml) chickpea liquid; discard remaining liquid.

3 Blend or process chickpeas with salt, garlic, tahini, juice and reserved liquid until almost smooth.

4 Spoon into serving bowl; sprinkle with pepper and parsley. Drizzle with olive oil.

makes 2 cups (470g)

per tablespoon 5.4g fat; 328kJ (78 cal)
serving suggestion Serve with warm pide or toasted pitta, or as an accompaniment to grilled kebabs or roast meat.

spanakopita   GREECE

PREPARATION TIME **40 MINUTES**   COOKING TIME **30 MINUTES**

For this recipe, use silverbeet, also known as swiss chard, rather than spinach.

1.5kg silverbeet, trimmed
1 tablespoon olive oil
1 medium brown onion (150g),
    chopped finely
2 cloves garlic, crushed
1 teaspoon ground nutmeg
200g fetta cheese, crumbled
1 tablespoon finely grated lemon rind
¼ cup chopped fresh mint
¼ cup chopped fresh flat-leaf parsley
¼ cup chopped fresh dill
4 green onions, chopped finely
16 sheets fillo pastry
125g butter, melted
2 teaspoons sesame seeds

1 Boil, steam or microwave silverbeet until just wilted; drain. Squeeze out excess moisture; drain on absorbent paper. Chop silverbeet coarsely; spread out on absorbent paper.

2 Heat oil in small frying pan; cook brown onion and garlic, stirring, until onion is soft. Add nutmeg; cook, stirring, until fragrant. Combine onion mixture and silverbeet in large bowl with fetta, rind, herbs and green onion.

3 Preheat oven to moderate. Brush one sheet of fillo with butter; fold lengthways into thirds, brushing with butter between each fold. Place rounded tablespoon of silverbeet mixture at the bottom of one narrow edge of folded fillo sheet, leaving a border. Fold opposite corner of fillo diagonally across the filling to form large triangle; continue folding to end of fillo sheet, retaining triangular shape. Place on lightly oiled oven tray, seam-side down; repeat with remaining ingredients.

4 Brush spanakopita with remaining butter; sprinkle with sesame seeds. Bake, uncovered, in moderate oven about 15 minutes or until browned lightly.

makes 16

per triangle 11.3g fat; 706kJ (169 cal)
serving suggestion Drizzle a mixture of chopped cucumber and yogurt over the top of the spanakopita.
tip To prevent fillo drying out, keep it covered with a damp tea-towel until ready to use.

empanadas MEXICO

PREPARATION TIME **30 MINUTES** COOKING TIME **1 HOUR** (plus cooling time)

These meat turnovers from Mexico take their name from the Spanish word empanar, which means to bake in pastry. Our empanadas are the perfect size for finger food.

400g can tomatoes
1 tablespoon olive oil
1 medium brown onion (150g),
   chopped finely
1 clove garlic, crushed
1 teaspoon cracked black pepper
½ teaspoon ground cinnamon
½ teaspoon ground clove
600g beef mince
¼ cup (40g) raisins, chopped coarsely
1 tablespoon cider vinegar
¼ cup (35g) toasted slivered almonds
2 x 800g packets ready-rolled
   quiche pastry
1 egg, beaten lightly
vegetable oil, for deep-frying

1 Blend or process undrained tomatoes until smooth; reserve.

2 Heat oil in large heavy-based saucepan; cook onion, garlic and spices, stirring, until onion is soft. Add beef; cook, stirring, until changed in colour. Drain away excess fat from pan. Stir in tomato, raisins and vinegar; simmer, uncovered, about 20 minutes or until mixture thickens. Stir in almonds; cool.

3 Cut 9cm rounds from each pastry sheet (you will need 32 rounds). Place a level tablespoon of beef mixture in centre of each round; brush edges lightly with egg. Fold pastry over to enclose filling, press edges together to seal.

4 Deep-fry empanadas in hot oil until crisp and browned lightly, drain on absorbent paper. Serve immediately with a dollop of sour cream or bottled salsa, if desired.

makes 32

per empanada 13.4g fat; 794kJ (190 cal)
serving suggestion If you'd like to serve empanadas as a meal, Spanish rice and refried beans make perfect accompaniments.
tip For a lower-fat version, empanadas can be baked, uncovered, in a preheated hot oven about 25 minutes or until browned.

marinated vegetables   ITALY

eggplants

PREPARATION TIME **15 MINUTES**
(plus standing time)
COOKING TIME **5 MINUTES**

Store in refrigerator for up to three months.

10 medium baby eggplants (600g)
coarse cooking salt
1 litre (4 cups) white vinegar
2 cups (500ml) water
2 teaspoons dried mint
½ teaspoon dried thyme
1 clove garlic, sliced finely
1 small fresh red chilli,
**   seeded, chopped**
½ teaspoon cracked black pepper
1½ cups (375ml) hot olive oil,
**   approximately**

1 Cut eggplants into quarters lengthways; place eggplant in colander, sprinkle with salt, stand 1 hour. Rinse eggplant under cold water; drain on absorbent paper.

2 Heat vinegar, the water and 2 teaspoons of salt in non-reactive pan until hot (do not boil). Add eggplant; simmer gently, uncovered, for 5 minutes, drain. Discard vinegar mixture.

3 Combine herbs, garlic, chilli, pepper and hot oil in heatproof bowl. Place eggplant upright in sterilised 1-litre (4 cup) jar; carefully top with enough oil mixture to cover eggplant, leaving 1cm space between eggplant and top of jar. Seal while hot.

makes 1 litre (4 cups)

per 100g 12.7g fat; 512kJ (122 cal)

mushrooms

PREPARATION TIME **10 MINUTES**
COOKING TIME **5 MINUTES**

Store in refrigerator for up to three months.

1 litre (4 cups) white vinegar
2 cups (500ml) water
2 teaspoons salt
800g button mushrooms
2 teaspoons dried parsley
½ teaspoon dried thyme
1 clove garlic, sliced finely
½ teaspoon cracked black pepper
1½ cups (375ml) hot olive oil,
**   approximately**

1 Heat vinegar, the water and salt in non-reactive pan until hot (do not boil). Add mushrooms; simmer gently, uncovered, for 5 minutes, drain. Discard vinegar mixture.

2 Combine hot mushrooms, herbs, garlic and pepper in large heatproof bowl; mix well. Pour hot oil over mushroom mixture, taking care, as it will bubble. Place mushroom mixture in sterilised 1-litre (4 cup) jar; top with enough oil to completely cover mushrooms, leaving 1cm space between mushrooms and top of jar. Seal while hot.

makes 1 litre (4 cups)

per 100g 10.8g fat; 452kJ (108 cal)

capsicums

PREPARATION TIME **20 MINUTES**
COOKING TIME **20 MINUTES**

Store in refrigerator for up to three months.

3 medium red capsicums (600g)
3 medium yellow capsicums (600g)
1 litre (4 cups) white vinegar
2 cups (500ml) water
2 teaspoons salt
1 clove garlic, sliced finely
½ teaspoon dried thyme
3 dried bay leaves
½ teaspoon cracked black pepper
1½ cups (375ml) hot olive oil,
**   approximately**

1 Remove seeds and membranes from capsicums; cut capsicum into 4cm strips. Heat vinegar, the water and salt in non-reactive pan until hot (do not boil). Add capsicum; simmer gently, uncovered, for 15 minutes, drain. Discard vinegar mixture.

2 Combine hot capsicum, garlic, thyme, bay leaves and pepper in large heatproof bowl. Add hot oil, taking care, as it will bubble. Place capsicum mixture in sterilised 1-litre (4 cup) jar; top with enough oil to cover capsicum, leaving 1cm space between capsicum and top of jar. Seal while hot.

makes 1 litre (4 cups)

per 100g 10.1g fat; 429kJ (102 cal)

felafel MIDDLE-EAST

PREPARATION TIME **45 MINUTES (plus standing time)** COOKING TIME **20 MINUTES**

2 cups (400g) dried chickpeas
1 medium brown onion (150g), chopped coarsely
2 cloves garlic, quartered
½ cup fresh flat-leaf parsley, chopped coarsely
2 teaspoons ground coriander
1 teaspoon ground cumin
1 teaspoon bicarbonate of soda
2 tablespoons plain flour
1 teaspoon salt
vegetable oil, for deep frying

1 Place chickpeas in large bowl, cover with cold water; stand overnight, drain.

2 Combine chickpeas, onion, garlic, parsley and spices in large bowl. Blend or process, in two batches, until almost smooth; return mixture to large bowl.

3 Add soda, flour and salt to chickpea mixture; knead on lightly floured surface for 2 minutes. Stand 30 minutes.

4 Roll level tablespoons of mixture into balls; stand 10 minutes. Deep-fry balls in hot oil, in batches, until golden brown. Serve with separate bowls of dukkah and yogurt for dipping, if desired.

makes 50

per felafel 1.1g fat; 124kJ (30 cal)

baba ghanoush MIDDLE-EAST

PREPARATION TIME **15 MINUTES (plus standing time)** COOKING TIME **1 HOUR**

Baba ghanoush, a Middle-Eastern puree of eggplant and tahini, is usually served as a dip, but can be served as a salad by adding lots of black olives and tomato slices. If you find the smoky flavour too strong, soften it by stirring in 1 tablespoon of yogurt. Tahini, a sesame seed paste, is available from selected supermarkets and delicatessens.

2 large eggplants (1kg)
¼ cup (70g) tahini
¼ cup (60ml) lemon juice
3 cloves garlic, quartered
1 teaspoon salt
1 tablespoon finely chopped
   fresh flat-leaf parsley

1 Preheat oven to hot.

2 Pierce eggplants all over with fork or skewer; place whole eggplants on oiled oven tray. Bake, uncovered, in hot oven about 1 hour or until soft. Stand 15 minutes.

3 Peel eggplants, discard skins; chop flesh coarsely.

4 Blend or process eggplant with tahini, juice, garlic and salt, until combined. Spoon into serving bowl; sprinkle with parsley.

makes 3 cups (700g)

per 100g 4.3g fat; 247kJ (59 cal)

serving suggestion Baba ghanoush is usually served as a dip, with pitta bread, but it's also delicious as a sandwich spread or as an accompaniment to roast lamb.

crab and prawn wontons   CHINA

PREPARATION TIME **1 HOUR** COOKING TIME **30 MINUTES**

Frozen wontons can be deep-fried as is;
freeze uncooked wontons in packs of 10,
so you can take only as many as you need
from the freezer.

500g uncooked prawns
500g crabmeat
1 teaspoon grated fresh ginger
1 clove garlic, crushed
4 green onions, chopped finely
1 tablespoon soy sauce
1 tablespoon sweet chilli sauce
80 wonton wrappers
1 tablespoon cornflour
1 tablespoon water
vegetable oil, for deep-frying

DIPPING SAUCE
2 teaspoons soy sauce
2 tablespoons sweet chilli sauce
1 teaspoon dry sherry
1 green onion, chopped finely

1 Shell and devein prawns; chop prawn meat finely.

2 Combine prawn meat in medium bowl with crab, ginger,
   garlic, onion and sauces.

3 Place 1 heaped teaspoon of prawn mixture in centre of
   each wrapper; brush edges with blended cornflour and
   water, pinch edges together to seal.

4 Deep-fry wontons in hot oil, in batches, until browned
   and cooked through. Drain on absorbent paper; serve
   with dipping sauce.

   dipping sauce Combine ingredients in small bowl.

makes 80

per wonton 1.1g fat; 113kJ (27 cal)
tip Canned crabmeat can be used; drain well.

fresh rice paper rolls with prawns   VIETNAM

PREPARATION TIME **25 MINUTES**   COOKING TIME **5 MINUTES** (plus cooling time)

You will need approximately a quarter of a small chinese cabbage for this recipe.

24 cooked medium prawns (650g)
1 cup (80g) finely shredded
   chinese cabbage
1 medium carrot (120g), grated
2 tablespoons chopped fresh mint
2 tablespoons chopped
   fresh coriander
12 x 16cm rice paper rounds

DIPPING SAUCE
⅓ cup (75g) caster sugar
¼ cup (60ml) white vinegar
¼ cup (60ml) water
2 teaspoons fish sauce
2 fresh red thai chillies, sliced thinly
1 tablespoon chopped fresh coriander

1 Shell and devein prawns.

2 Combine cabbage, carrot, mint and coriander in medium bowl. Place one rice paper round in medium bowl of warm water until softened slightly; lift sheet carefully from water. Place on board; pat dry with absorbent paper.

3 Place a twelfth of the cabbage mixture in centre of rice paper round; top with two prawns. Fold in sides; roll to enclose filling. Repeat with remaining rice paper rounds, cabbage mixture and prawns. Serve rolls with dipping sauce.

dipping sauce Stir sugar, vinegar and the water in small saucepan over heat until sugar dissolves; bring to a boil. Remove from heat, stir in sauce and chilli; cool. Stir in coriander.

makes 12

per roll 0.3g fat; 222kJ (53 cal)
tip Cover rolls with a damp towel to help prevent the rice paper from drying out.

samosas with coriander yogurt   INDIA

PREPARATION TIME **1 HOUR 30 MINUTES (plus standing time)** COOKING TIME **30 MINUTES (plus cooling time)**

The filling and pastry can be made a day ahead. Cooked samosas are suitable to freeze; potato and kumara are suitable to microwave. Ghee is clarified butter, and is available from supermarkets.

3 cups (450g) plain flour
1 teaspoon salt
60g ghee
¾ cup (180ml) cold water, approximately
1 small potato (120g), chopped finely
1 small kumara (250g), chopped finely
20g ghee, extra
1 small brown onion (80g), chopped
1 clove garlic, crushed
1 teaspoon finely grated fresh ginger
1 teaspoon ground cumin
1 teaspoon ground coriander
½ teaspoon black mustard seeds
½ cup (60g) frozen peas, thawed
vegetable oil, for deep-frying

CORIANDER YOGURT
½ teaspoon cumin seeds
1 cup (280g) yogurt
½ cup fresh mint leaves
½ cup fresh coriander leaves
¼ teaspoon cayenne pepper
1 tablespoon lemon juice

1 Sift flour and salt into a medium bowl; rub in ghee until mixture resembles fine breadcrumbs. Add enough of the water to mix to a soft dough. Knead dough on a lightly floured surface for about 10 minutes or until smooth and elastic. Cover with plastic wrap and stand at room temperature for 1 hour.

2 Meanwhile, boil, steam or microwave combined potato and kumara until just tender; mash half of the potato mixture until almost smooth.

3 Heat extra ghee in large frying pan; cook onion, garlic, ginger and spices, stirring, until onion is soft and spices fragrant. Add both potato mixtures and peas; cook, stirring, until well combined, cool.

4 Divide dough into quarters; roll each piece on a floured surface until as thin as possible (approximately 2mm). Cut into 9cm rounds, put 2 teaspoons of filling in centre of each pastry round, wet edge lightly with water. Fold pastry in half to enclose filling. Pinch edge of pastry with thumb and index finger, fold pastry over the unpinched edge, pinch down again; repeat around edge of the pastry. Repeat with remaining pastry and filling.

5 Deep-fry samosas, in batches, in hot oil until browned; drain on absorbent paper. Serve with coriander yogurt.

coriander yogurt   Add seeds to heated frying pan; cook over medium heat, shaking pan, until the seeds are fragrant. Blend or process seeds and remaining ingredients until almost smooth.

makes 36

per samosa 4.5g fat; 389kJ (93 cal)

dolmades   GREECE

PREPARATION TIME 30 MINUTES   COOKING TIME 1 HOUR 20 MINUTES (plus cooling time)

Vine leaves are available from delicatessens and supermarkets. This recipe can be made four days ahead; store, covered, in refrigerator.

300g packet vine leaves in brine
1 tablespoon lemon juice
¾ cup (180ml) water
1 tablespoon olive oil

FILLING
¼ cup (60ml) olive oil
1 medium brown onion (150g),
  chopped finely
2 tablespoons pine nuts
½ cup (100g) short-grain rice
2 tablespoons currants
½ cup (125ml) water
2 tablespoons finely chopped
  fresh flat-leaf parsley

1 Rinse vine leaves under cold water; drain well. Place vine leaves vein-side-up on bench, place 2 level teaspoons of filling on each leaf; roll up firmly, folding in sides, to enclose filling.

2 Place rolls in single layer in heavy-based medium saucepan, add combined juice, water and oil. Place a plate on top of rolls to keep rolls in position during cooking. Simmer, covered, over low heat 1 hour.

filling Heat oil in medium saucepan, add onion; cook, stirring, until soft. Add nuts; cook, stirring, until lightly browned. Stir in rice and currants, mix well to coat rice in oil. Add water; simmer, covered, over low heat about 10 minutes or until liquid is absorbed. Remove pan from heat; cool mixture. Stir in parsley.

makes 24

per roll 3.9g fat; 222kJ (53 cal)

taramasalata GREECE

PREPARATION TIME 10 MINUTES COOKING TIME 15 MINUTES (plus cooling time)

This recipe can be made three days ahead; store, covered, in the refrigerator.

1 large old potato (300g), peeled, chopped
100g tarama
1 tablespoon lemon juice
¼ cup (60ml) white vinegar
½ small white onion (40g), grated finely
¾ cup (180ml) extra light olive oil

1 Boil, steam or microwave potato until tender; cool, refrigerate until cold.

2 Mash potato with remaining ingredients until smooth.

makes 2½ cups (600g)

per tablespoon 8.6g fat; 368kJ (88 cal)

tzatziki GREECE

PREPARATION TIME **10 MINUTES** (plus refrigeration and standing time)

Tzatziki, a yogurt and cucumber dip, makes the perfect start to a great Greek meal. This recipe can be made a day ahead; store, covered, in the refrigerator.

500g greek-style yogurt or plain yogurt
1 lebanese cucumber (130g),
**   peeled, grated coarsely**
½ teaspoon salt
1 clove garlic, crushed
1 tablespoon lemon juice
2 tablespoons shredded fresh mint

1 Place yogurt onto large square of double-thickness muslin cloth. Tie the ends of the cloth together and hang it over a large bowl, or place in a sieve. Refrigerate about 2 hours or until the yogurt is thick.

2 Meanwhile, combine the cucumber and salt in a small bowl and stand for 20 minutes. Gently squeeze out excess liquid.

3 Combine yogurt, cucumber, garlic, juice and mint in a small bowl; mix well.

makes 1¾ cups (410g)

per tablespoon 1.7g fat; 104kJ (25 cal)

tuna sashimi   JAPAN

PREPARATION TIME **10 MINUTES (plus soaking time)**

The most important step to successful sashimi making is the guarantee that you start with the freshest of fish. Use a mandoline (if you own one) to shred the daikon (a Japanese radish). You'll need a piece of daikon about 7cm long and 5cm in diameter for this recipe.

¾ cup (200g) finely shredded daikon
400g sashimi tuna
2 teaspoons wasabi
2 tablespoons pink pickled ginger
⅓ cup (80ml) japanese soy sauce

1 Soak daikon in bowl of iced water for 15 minutes; drain well.

2 Place tuna on chopping board; using very sharp knife, cut 6mm slices at right angles to the grain of the fish, holding the piece of skinned fish with your fingers and slicing with the knife almost vertical to the board.

3 Divide tuna slices among serving dishes; mound equal amounts of daikon next to tuna.

4 Garnish plates with equal amounts of mounded wasabi and pickled ginger; serve with separate bowls of soy sauce.

serves 4

per serving 5.8g fat; 706kJ (169 cal)

chicken liver and port pâté   FRANCE

PREPARATION TIME **50 MINUTES (plus standing and refrigeration time)** COOKING TIME **15 MINUTES**

500g chicken livers
⅓ cup (80ml) port
⅓ cup (80ml) olive oil
1 small white onion (80g),
   chopped finely
1 clove garlic, crushed
⅓ cup (80ml) cream
½ teaspoon ground thyme
1 teaspoon gelatine
¼ cup (60ml) water
fresh thyme sprigs

1 Trim and wash livers; cut livers in half. Place liver in small bowl with port; stand 2 hours. Strain liver, reserve liquid.

2 Heat half of the oil in medium frying pan, add onion and garlic; stir over heat until onion is soft. Add liver to pan; stir over heat about 2 minutes or until liver just changes colour. Add reserved liquid; simmer, uncovered, 1 minute.

3 Blend or process liver mixture, cream and ground thyme until smooth. Add remaining oil while motor is operating, process until smooth. Pour into 3-cup (750ml) serving dish, cover; refrigerate 2 hours.

4 Sprinkle gelatine over the water in heatproof jug, stand in small saucepan of simmering water; stir until dissolved, cool to room temperature. Arrange fresh thyme on pâté, carefully pour gelatine mixture over pâté; cover, refrigerate overnight.

serves 4

per serving 31.9g fat; 1735kJ (415 cal)
serving suggestion Serve with thin toasted slices of french bread.
tip If preferred, you can top pâté with lemon and lime slices, orange slices, bay leaves, sliced green olives or other fresh herbs, in place of the thyme sprigs.

soups

From the clear, steaming broths of China, Vietnam and Thailand to creamy, piping-hot bowls of comfort from France, England and the USA, soup proves itself a global favourite again and again.

scotch broth SCOTLAND

PREPARATION TIME **20 MINUTES** COOKING TIME **2 HOURS**

This soup, a rich lamb stock with root vegetables and barley, can also have ½ cup (125ml) dry white wine added along with the water.

6 lamb neck chops (1kg)
2 litres (8 cups) water
¾ cup (150g) pearl barley
1 medium brown onion (150g),
　chopped coarsely
2 medium carrots (240g),
　chopped coarsely
1 medium leek (350g),
　chopped coarsely
2 turnips (430g), trimmed,
　chopped coarsely
2 cups (160g) finely shredded
　savoy cabbage
⅔ cup (100g) frozen peas
2 tablespoons chopped fresh
　flat-leaf parsley

1 Combine lamb, the water and barley in large saucepan. Bring to a boil; simmer, covered, 1 hour, skimming fat from surface occasionally.

2 Add onion, carrot, leek and turnip; simmer, covered, about 40 minutes or until vegetables are tender.

3 Remove lamb from soup; remove meat from bones, discard bones, coarsely chop meat.

4 Return lamb to soup with cabbage and peas; cook, uncovered, 10 minutes.

5 Just before serving, stir in parsley.

serves 6

per serving 11.9g fat; 1404kJ (336 cal)
serving suggestion Serve with cheese scones.
tip Any root vegetable can be used in this soup.

gazpacho SPAIN

PREPARATION TIME **30 MINUTES (plus refrigeration time)**

A chilled soup originating in the southern province of Andalusia in Spain, gazpacho, like other peasant soups, makes clever use of the garden's overripe vegetables.

1 litre (4 cups) tomato juice
10 medium egg tomatoes (750g), chopped coarsely
2 medium red onions (340g), chopped coarsely
2 cloves garlic, quartered
1 lebanese cucumber (130g), chopped coarsely
2 tablespoons sherry vinegar
1 medium red capsicum (200g), chopped coarsely
1 small red onion (100g), chopped finely, extra
1 lebanese cucumber (130g), chopped finely, extra
1 small red capsicum (150g), chopped finely, extra
1 tablespoon chopped fresh dill

1 Blend or process juice, tomato, onion, garlic, cucumber, vinegar and capsicum, in batches, until pureed. Cover; refrigerate 3 hours.

2 Just before serving, divide soup among serving bowls; stir equal amounts of combined extra onion, extra cucumber, extra capsicum and dill into each bowl.

serves 6

per serving 0.4g fat; 368kJ (88 cal)

serving suggestion To make this soup a complete meal, add ½ cup of both finely chopped raw celery and finely chopped green capsicum to the soup, then top each serving with 1 tablespoon of finely diced hard-boiled egg and a few croutons.

tips A finely chopped red chilli added to the blender or processor makes a spicier gazpacho.

Red wine vinegar can be used instead of sherry vinegar.

tom ka gai   THAILAND

PREPARATION TIME **20 MINUTES**   COOKING TIME **30 MINUTES**

This is the traditional creamy coconut and chicken soup we've all eaten at our local Thai restaurant – now you can make it yourself and enjoy it more often.

2 teaspoons peanut oil
1 tablespoon finely chopped
    fresh lemon grass
1 tablespoon grated
    fresh galangal
2 teaspoons grated
    fresh ginger
1 clove garlic, crushed
3 red thai chillies, seeded,
    chopped finely
4 kaffir lime leaves,
    sliced finely
¼ teaspoon ground turmeric
2⅔ cups (660ml) coconut milk
1 litre (4 cups) chicken stock
2 cups (500ml) water
1 tablespoon fish sauce
500g chicken thigh fillets,
    sliced thinly
3 green onions,
    chopped finely
2 tablespoons lime juice
1 tablespoon chopped
    fresh coriander

1 Heat oil in large saucepan; cook lemon grass, galangal, ginger, garlic, chilli, lime leaves and turmeric, stirring, about 2 minutes or until fragrant.

2 Stir in coconut milk, stock, the water and fish sauce; bring to a boil. Add chicken; simmer, uncovered, about 20 minutes or until chicken is cooked through and soup liquid reduced slightly.

3 Just before serving, stir onion, juice and coriander into soup.

serves 6

per serving 30.8g fat; 1655kJ (396 cal)
serving suggestions Serve with a side plate of fresh mint leaves, bean spouts and lime wedges.
tip Remove all excess fat from chicken before cooking.

hot and sour soup CHINA

PREPARATION TIME **25 MINUTES (plus standing time)** COOKING TIME **2 HOURS 30 MINUTES**

This hot and sour soup originated in the Sichuan province of western China, where it helps lend warmth on cold days.

1.5kg chicken bones
4 litres (16 cups) water
2 medium brown onions (300g),
   chopped coarsely
2 trimmed celery sticks (150g),
   chopped coarsely
1 large carrot (180g), chopped coarsely
1 tablespoon sichuan peppercorns
3 bay leaves
340g chicken breast fillets
6 dried shiitake mushrooms
225g can bamboo shoots, drained, sliced thinly
50g piece fresh ginger, sliced thinly
2 teaspoons sesame oil
2 tablespoons cider vinegar
2 tablespoons sweet chilli sauce
¼ cup (60ml) soy sauce
150g rice stick noodles
4 green onions, sliced thinly

1 Combine chicken bones with the water, brown onion, celery, carrot, peppercorns and bay leaves in large saucepan. Bring to a boil; simmer, uncovered, 1½ hours, skimming occasionally.

2 Add chicken breast; simmer, uncovered, about 20 minutes or until chicken is cooked through. Strain through muslin-lined strainer into large bowl. Reserve stock and chicken; discard bones and vegetables. When chicken is cool enough to handle, shred finely.

3 Meanwhile, place mushrooms in small heatproof bowl, cover with boiling water, stand 10 minutes; drain. Remove and discard stems from mushrooms; slice caps thinly.

4 Return stock to same cleaned pan with mushrooms, bamboo shoots, ginger, oil, vinegar and sauces; bring to a boil. Simmer, uncovered, 15 minutes, stirring occasionally. Add shredded chicken and noodles; cook, stirring, about 5 minutes or until noodles are just tender.

5 Just before serving, add green onion to soup.

serves 6

per serving 4.5g fat; 686kJ (164 cal)
tip You can use chicken necks or wings to make the stock, rather than the chicken bones.

pho VIETNAM

PREPARATION TIME 20 MINUTES (plus cooling time) COOKING TIME 30 MINUTES

You will need 1 bunch of fresh coriander for this recipe.

3 litres (12 cups) chicken stock
60g piece fresh ginger, peeled,
**   sliced thinly**
2 tablespoons fish sauce
2 cloves garlic, quartered
½ cup coarsely chopped fresh
**   coriander roots**
1 star anise
340g chicken breast fillets,
**   sliced thinly**
400g dried rice stick noodles
12 green onions, sliced
3 cups (240g) bean sprouts
½ cup loosely packed fresh
**   vietnamese mint leaves**
½ cup loosely packed fresh
**   coriander leaves**
sambal oelek, to serve
1 medium lemon (140g),
**   cut into wedges**

1 Place combined stock, ginger, sauce, garlic, coriander roots and star anise in large saucepan. Bring to a boil; simmer, uncovered, 10 minutes. Strain stock into a large heatproof jug or bowl and discard ginger, coriander roots, garlic and star anise.

2 Return stock to pan, add chicken; simmer, uncovered, about 5 minutes or until chicken is cooked through.

3 Meanwhile, cook noodles in large saucepan of boiling water until tender. Drain well. Divide noodles, green onion and bean sprouts among serving bowls; pour hot soup over and top with mint leaves and coriander leaves. Serve with sambal and lemon.

serves 6

per serving 4.4g fat; 1436kJ (343 cal)
tips Star anise are dried, star-shaped pods with an aniseed flavour, available from Asian and gourmet food stores.
Chicken is easier to slice thinly while it is partially frozen.

vichyssoise FRANCE

PREPARATION TIME **15 MINUTES (plus refrigeration time)** COOKING TIME **40 MINUTES**

Vichyssoise is a well-known French potato and leek soup; rich and creamy, it is generally served cold.

60g butter
1 large brown onion (200g),
  chopped finely
2 medium leeks (700g), sliced thinly
3 large potatoes (900g),
  chopped coarsely
4 trimmed celery sticks (300g),
  chopped coarsely
2 litres (8 cups) chicken stock
¾ cup (180ml) cream
2 tablespoons chopped fresh chervil

1 Melt butter in large saucepan; cook onion, stirring, until onion is soft. Add leek; cook, stirring, about 10 minutes or until leek is soft.

2 Add potato and celery; cook, stirring, 2 minutes. Stir in stock, bring to a boil; simmer, uncovered, about 15 minutes or until potato is soft, stirring occasionally.

3 Blend or process soup, in batches, adding cream gradually, until smooth. Cover; refrigerate 3 hours or overnight.

4 Just before serving, stir chervil through cold soup.

serves 6

per serving 22g fat; 1572kJ (376 cal)
serving suggestion This soup can also be served hot with garlic croutons.
tips Both the leek and potato must be cooked until very soft for the requisite smoothness of this soup.
We recommend you use homemade stock for this delicate soup.

tom yum goong THAILAND

PREPARATION TIME 30 MINUTES COOKING TIME 20 MINUTES

This is probably the Thai soup most favoured by Westerners. Sour and tangy, tom yum goong can easily become a main meal by adding more prawns to the basic recipe. You will need about two medium limes for this recipe.

1.5 litres (6 cups) fish stock
1 bunch fresh coriander
1 tablespoon chopped fresh
    lemon grass
4 fresh kaffir lime leaves, torn
40g fresh ginger, peeled, sliced thinly
4 red thai chillies, seeded, sliced thinly
1 tablespoon fish sauce
16 uncooked medium prawns (400g)
8 green onions
⅓ cup (80ml) fresh lime juice
1 teaspoon chilli paste
½ cup loosely packed fresh
    thai basil leaves

1   Heat stock, uncovered, in large saucepan.

2   Meanwhile, cut off coriander roots, add to stock in pan. Pick coriander leaves off stems; you will need ⅔ cup loosely packed coriander leaves.

3   Add lemon grass, lime leaves, ginger, chilli and sauce to stock, bring to a boil; simmer, uncovered, 10 minutes.

4   Meanwhile, shell and devein prawns, leaving heads and tails intact. Chop green onions into 2cm lengths. Remove and discard coriander roots from stock mixture. Add prawns, green onion, juice and paste to pan; simmer, uncovered, about 4 minutes or until prawns just change in colour. Add coriander leaves and basil leaves; serve immediately.

serves 4

per serving   0.9g fat; 581kJ (139 cal)

tip   We used a hot Vietnamese chilli paste here, but you can use sambal oelek or, for less heat, mild sweet chilli sauce.

pea and ham soup ENGLAND

PREPARATION TIME **15 MINUTES** COOKING TIME **2 HOURS**

Blue boilers – or field peas – are a special variety of pea grown specifically for being dried and used whole; when dried and halved, they're called split peas.

2 cups (375g) dried peas (blue boilers)
1 medium brown onion (150g),
chopped coarsely
2 trimmed celery sticks (150g),
chopped coarsely
2 bay leaves
1.5kg ham bone
2.5 litres (10 cups) water
1 teaspoon cracked black pepper

1 Combine ingredients in large saucepan. Bring to a boil; simmer, covered, about 2 hours or until peas are tender.

2 Remove ham bone; when cool enough to handle, remove ham from bone, shred finely. Discard bone and fat; remove and discard bay leaves.

3 Blend or process half of the pea mixture, in batches, until pureed; return to pan with remaining unprocessed pea mixture and ham. Reheat soup, stirring over heat until hot.

serves 6

per serving 4.2g fat; 1179kJ (282 cal)
serving suggestion Serve with homemade sourdough croutons.

borscht RUSSIA

PREPARATION TIME **30 MINUTES** COOKING TIME **1 HOUR 30 MINUTES**

One of the most famous of all Russian soups, borscht can be served hot or cold, pureed or chunky, meatless or replete with shredded beef, chicken or pork. This version is based on a strong-flavoured beef stock, acidulated with lemon or vinegar, and always served hot.

2kg (about 6) fresh beetroot
50g butter
2 medium brown onions (300g), chopped finely
2 medium potatoes (400g), chopped coarsely
400g can tomatoes
2 medium carrots (240g), chopped coarsely
2.5 litres (10 cups) water
⅓ cup (80ml) red wine vinegar
500g piece gravy beef
3 bay leaves
4 cups (320g) shredded savoy cabbage
½ cup (120g) sour cream
2 tablespoons chopped fresh flat-leaf parsley

1 Discard beetroot leaves and stems; peel and coarsely grate raw beetroot.

2 Melt butter in large saucepan; cook onion, stirring, until soft. Add beetroot, potato, undrained crushed tomatoes, carrot, the water, vinegar, beef and bay leaves. Bring to a boil; simmer, covered, 1 hour.

3 Remove and discard fat from surface of soup mixture. Remove beef from soup, shred beef then return to soup with cabbage; simmer, uncovered, 20 minutes.

4 Remove and discard bay leaves; ladle soup into serving bowls. Divide sour cream and parsley among bowls.

serves 6

per serving 22.6g fat; 1931kJ (462 cal)
serving suggestion Serve with warm homemade potato and caraway bread.
tip To avoid staining your hands, wear disposable kitchen gloves when peeling beetroot, then grate it using a food processor.

minestrone   ITALY

PREPARATION TIME **20 MINUTES**   COOKING TIME **45 MINUTES**

Minestrone comes from the word minestra, the first course of an Italian meal, and it has come to mean any chunky, rustic soup.

1 tablespoon olive oil
4 bacon rashers (280g), chopped coarsely
2 medium brown onions (300g), sliced thickly
2 cloves garlic, crushed
1 medium carrot (120g), chopped coarsely
2 small potatoes (240g), chopped coarsely
2 trimmed celery sticks (150g), chopped coarsely
1.5 litres (6 cups) beef stock
400g can tomatoes
2 tablespoons tomato paste
1 cup (150g) macaroni
½ cup (60g) frozen peas
1 cup (80g) finely shredded cabbage
2 small zucchini (180g), chopped coarsely

1 Heat oil in large saucepan; cook bacon, onion, garlic, carrot, potato and celery, stirring, until onion is soft.

2 Add stock, undrained crushed tomatoes and paste; bring to a boil. Simmer, covered, about 30 minutes or until vegetables are tender, stirring occasionally.

3 Add pasta, peas, cabbage and zucchini; boil, uncovered, about 10 minutes or until pasta is just tender.

serves 4

per serving 8.9g fat; 1559kJ (373 cal)
serving suggestions Don't forget to pass around a bowl of freshly grated parmesan cheese for diners to sprinkle over their soup. A crisp, hot loaf of ciabatta, sliced, is perfect for dipping in the soup.

bouillabaisse

FRANCE

PREPARATION TIME **35 MINUTES**
COOKING TIME **45 MINUTES**

Originating on the Mediterranean coast around Marseilles, this classic French dish was originally made by local fishermen with what was unsold of their daily catch. Rouille, a red sauce made with capsicums and chillies, and aïoli, that intense garlic mayonnaise, traditionally accompany bouillabaisse wherever it is served.

500g mussels
1kg scampi
2 tablespoons olive oil
2 small leeks (400g),
    chopped finely
1 large fennel bulb (650g),
    sliced thinly
2 cloves garlic, crushed
1 red thai chilli, seeded,
    chopped finely
6 medium tomatoes (1.2kg),
    peeled, chopped coarsely
2 litres (8 cups) fish stock
6 saffron threads
400g firm white fish fillets,
    chopped coarsely
200g scallops
2 tablespoons chopped fresh
    flat-leaf parsley

AIOLI
4 cloves garlic, quartered
2 egg yolks
2 tablespoons lemon juice
1 cup (250ml) olive oil

ROUILLE
2 medium red capsicums (400g)
2 red thai chillies, seeded,
    chopped coarsely
1 clove garlic, quartered
2 tablespoons stale breadcrumbs
¼ cup (60ml) olive oil

1 Scrub mussels under cold water; remove beards. Shell and devein half of the scampi; remove heads from remaining half.

2 Heat oil in large heavy-based saucepan; cook leek, fennel, garlic and chilli, stirring, about 10 minutes or until leek softens. Add tomato, stock and saffron; bring to a boil. Simmer, uncovered, about 20 minutes or until tomato is pulpy, stirring occasionally. Strain mixture into large clean saucepan; discard vegetables.

3 Bring stock mixture to a boil. Add mussels and scampi; simmer, covered, about 10 minutes or until mussels open (discard any that do not).

4 Add fish and scallops to pan; simmer, uncovered, 5 minutes. Just before serving, stir in parsley. Serve with aïoli and rouille.

aïoli Blend or process garlic, egg yolks and juice until creamy. With motor operating, gradually add oil; process until aïoli thickens.

rouille Quarter capsicums, remove and discard seeds and membranes. Roast under grill or in very hot oven, skin-side up, until skin blisters and blackens. Cover capsicum pieces with plastic or paper for 5 minutes; peel away skin, chop coarsely. Process capsicum, chilli, garlic and breadcrumbs until combined. With motor operating, gradually add oil; process until rouille thickens.

serves 6

per serving 67.6g fat; 3720kJ (890 cal)
serving suggestion Serve with a fresh crisp baguette.
tip Use your favourite seafood in this recipe. Squid, prawns or crab are tasty substitutions, and any sort of fish fillets can be used.

french onion soup FRANCE

PREPARATION TIME **25 MINUTES** COOKING TIME **35 MINUTES**

This classic soup became famous almost a hundred years ago as the early morning staple of Parisian workers in Les Halles markets. Its restorative qualities became appreciated among late-night revellers winding down at the markets, then spread to the vast hordes of tourists that descended on the French capital after the war. One of the easiest soups imaginable to make, you'll soon discover why it became – and has remained – so popular.

50g butter
6 medium brown onions (900g),
 sliced thickly
4 cloves garlic, crushed
½ cup (125ml) dry red wine
2 litres (8 cups) beef stock
4 sprigs fresh thyme
2 bay leaves
1 small french bread stick
1 cup (125g) coarsely grated
 gruyère cheese

1 Melt butter in large saucepan; cook onion and garlic, stirring, about 15 minutes or until onion caramelises.

2 Stir in wine, stock, thyme and bay leaves. Bring to a boil; simmer, uncovered, 20 minutes, stirring occasionally.

3 Meanwhile, cut bread into 2cm slices, place bread on oven tray; toast under hot grill until browned lightly both sides. Divide cheese among toasted bread slices; grill until cheese melts and is browned lightly.

4 Remove and discard bay leaves from soup. Just before serving, divide cheese toasts among serving bowls; pour hot onion soup over the toasts.

serves 6

per serving 14.6g fat; 1212kJ (290 cal)
serving suggestion Serve with a good bottle of red wine.
tip While gruyère is the traditional cheese of choice, you can substitute it with emmenthaler or jarlsberg.

prawn laksa   MALAYSIA

PREPARATION TIME **35 MINUTES** COOKING TIME **40 MINUTES**

1kg medium uncooked prawns
⅓ cup (90g) laksa paste
2¼ cups (560ml) coconut milk
1.25 litres (5 cups) chicken stock
2 red thai chillies, seeded,
**   chopped finely**
¼ cup (60ml) lime juice
1 tablespoon brown sugar
6 fresh vietnamese mint leaves, torn
250g dried rice noodles
vegetable oil, for shallow-frying
300g fresh firm tofu,
**   cut into 2cm cubes**
2½ cups (200g) bean sprouts
2 green onions, chopped finely

1 Shell and devein prawns, leaving tails intact.

2 Heat large dry saucepan; cook paste, stirring, until fragrant. Stir in milk, stock, chilli, juice, sugar and leaves. Bring to a boil; simmer, covered, 30 minutes.

3 Meanwhile, cook noodles in large saucepan of boiling water, uncovered, until just tender; drain. Heat oil in wok or large heavy-based frying pan; cook tofu, in batches, until browned all over. Drain on absorbent paper.

4 Add prawns to laksa mixture; simmer, uncovered, about 5 minutes or until prawns are just changed in colour.

5 Just before serving, add noodles, tofu, sprouts and onion to pan; stir gently until ingredients are just combined and laksa is hot.

serves 4

per serving 48g fat; 3523kJ (843 cal)
tips Don't seed the chillies if you like your laksa hot, or serve it, as they do in Malaysia, with a bowl of sambal oelek.
Omit the prawns in this recipe and substitute chopped, cooked chicken or, for a vegetable version, chopped baby bok choy, spinach or cabbage.

fish chowder   USA

PREPARATION TIME **20 MINUTES**   COOKING TIME **40 MINUTES**

600g boneless white fish fillets
50g butter
2 cloves garlic, crushed
1 small leek (200g), sliced thinly
2 bacon rashers (140g), chopped finely
1 trimmed celery stick (75g),
**   chopped finely**
1 cup (250ml) dry white wine
1 tablespoon plain flour
3 medium potatoes (500g),
**   cut into 1.5cm cubes**
3 cups (750ml) milk
300ml cream
2 tablespoons coarsely chopped
**   fresh flat-leaf parsley**

1 Place fish fillets in large frying pan with enough water to cover; bring to a boil. Reduce heat; simmer, uncovered, about 5 minutes or until fish fillets are cooked through, drain. Remove bones from fish, break into large pieces, reserve.

2 Meanwhile, melt butter in large heavy-based saucepan; cook garlic and leek, stirring, until leek softens. Add bacon and celery; cook, stirring, until bacon is browned and crisp.

3 Add wine, bring to a boil; cook, stirring occasionally, until wine has reduced by about a third. Add flour; cook, stirring, 1 minute. Add potato and milk; simmer, uncovered, about 20 minutes or until potato is just tender.

4 Stir in cream; simmer until potato is just tender. Add reserved fish, cook until heated through. Add parsley just before serving.

serves 4

per serving   47.6g fat; 3214kJ (769 cal)
serving suggestion   Serve with fresh sourdough rolls.

combination noodle soup　CHINA

PREPARATION TIME **15 MINUTES**　COOKING TIME **30 MINUTES**

500g chicken breast fillets
2 litres (8 cups) chicken stock
1 tablespoon light soy sauce
125g fresh thin wheat noodles
100g small cooked shelled prawns
200g chinese barbecued pork,
　sliced thinly
1¼ cups (100g) bean sprouts
4 green onions, sliced

1　Poach chicken in simmering water about 15 minutes or until cooked through.

2　Remove chicken from pan using a slotted spoon; when cool enough to handle, slice chicken thinly.

3　Combine stock and soy sauce in large saucepan, cover; bring to a boil.

4　Add noodles to boiling stock; using tongs or a large metal fork, immediately separate the strands. Reduce heat, add chicken, prawns, pork, sprouts and onion to pan; simmer soup until heated through.

5　Using tongs, lift noodles from soup; divide among serving bowls. Ladle remaining soup over noodles.

serves 4

per serving　14.9g fat; 1563kJ (374 cal)

mains

Classic main courses vary enormously from country to country... consider the contrast between Hungarian goulash, India's famous vindaloo, the noodle-based pad thai and an authentic Spanish paella. Curries, roasts, tempuras and tagines – each has its place in this expansive chapter.

roast beef with yorkshire puddings   ENGLAND

PREPARATION TIME 35 MINUTES (plus refrigeration and standing time) COOKING TIME 2 HOURS

2kg corner piece beef topside roast
2 cups (500ml) dry red wine
2 bay leaves
6 black peppercorns
¼ cup (70g) wholegrain mustard
4 cloves garlic, sliced
4 sprigs fresh thyme
1 medium brown onion (150g),
    chopped coarsely
2 medium carrots (240g),
    chopped coarsely
1 large leek (500g), chopped coarsely
2 trimmed sticks celery (150g),
    chopped coarsely
2 tablespoons olive oil
2 tablespoons plain flour
1½ cups (375ml) beef stock

YORKSHIRE PUDDINGS
1 cup (150g) plain flour
½ teaspoon salt
2 eggs, beaten lightly
½ cup (125ml) milk
½ cup (125ml) water

1 Combine beef, wine, bay leaves, peppercorns, mustard, garlic, thyme and onion in large bowl, cover; refrigerate 3 hours or overnight.

2 Preheat oven to moderate. Drain beef over medium bowl; reserve 1 cup (250ml) of marinade. Combine carrot, leek and celery in large baking dish, top with beef; brush beef with oil.

3 Bake, uncovered, in moderate oven about 1½ hours or until browned and cooked as desired.

4 Remove beef from pan, wrap in foil; stand 20 minutes before serving. Remove vegetables with slotted spoon; discard vegetables. Pour pan juices into jug, stand 2 minutes, then pour off excess oil; reserve 1½ tablespoons oil for yorkshire puddings and 2 tablespoons of pan juices for gravy.

5 Heat reserved pan juices for gravy in same baking dish, add flour; cook, stirring, until bubbling. Gradually add reserved marinade and stock; cook, stirring, until mixture boils and thickens, strain gravy into jug. Serve beef with yorkshire puddings and gravy, and roasted potatoes and greens, if desired.

yorkshire puddings Sift flour and salt into bowl, make well in centre; add combined egg, milk and water all at once. Using wooden spoon, gradually stir in flour from side of bowl until batter is smooth. Cover; allow to stand 30 minutes. Divide the reserved oil among 16 holes of mini (1½ tablespoons/30ml) muffin pans; heat in hot oven 2 minutes. Divide batter among pan holes. Bake in hot oven about 10 minutes or until puddings are puffed and golden.

serves 8

per serving 24g fat; 2424kJ (580 cal)

beef burritos   MEXICO

PREPARATION TIME **20 MINUTES**   COOKING TIME **35 MINUTES**

4 x 25cm-round flour tortillas
1 cup (125g) grated cheddar cheese
1 teaspoon hot paprika
¾ cup (180g) sour cream
1 tablespoon chopped fresh coriander

BEAN AND BEEF FILLING
1 tablespoon olive oil
500g beef mince
1 medium brown onion (150g),
  chopped finely
1 clove garlic, crushed
400g can tomatoes
35g packet taco seasoning mix
½ cup (125ml) water
300g can kidney beans, rinsed, drained

1 Preheat oven to moderately hot.

2 Divide warm bean and beef filling among tortillas, roll; secure with toothpicks.

3 Place filled tortillas on oiled oven tray; sprinkle with cheese and paprika. Bake in moderately hot oven about 10 minutes or until heated through.

4 Remove toothpicks; serve topped with sour cream, coriander and, if desired, guacamole (see recipe page 10).

bean and beef filling Heat oil in medium frying pan; cook beef, stirring, until browned. Add onion and garlic; cook, stirring, until onion is soft. Stir in undrained crushed tomatoes and remaining ingredients; simmer, uncovered, about 15 minutes or until mixture is thickened.

serves 4

per serving 50.2g fat; 3179kJ (759 cal)

tips The burritos must be assembled just before serving. The bean and beef filling can be made a day ahead and stored, covered, in the refrigerator.

chilli con carne   USA

PREPARATION TIME 25 MINUTES (plus standing time)   COOKING TIME 3 HOURS 40 MINUTES (plus cooling time)

1 cup (200g) dried kidney beans
1.5kg beef chuck steak
2 litres (8 cups) water
1 tablespoon olive oil
2 medium brown onions (300g),
    chopped coarsely
2 cloves garlic, crushed
2 teaspoons ground cumin
2 teaspoons ground coriander
½ teaspoon cayenne pepper
2 teaspoons sweet paprika
2 x 400g cans tomatoes
1 tablespoon tomato paste
4 green onions, chopped coarsely
2 tablespoons chopped
    fresh coriander
⅓ cup (65g) finely chopped,
    bottled jalapeño chillies

JALAPENO CORN MUFFINS
1 cup (150g) plain flour
1 teaspoon baking powder
2 cups (340g) polenta
2 teaspoons salt
1 cup (250ml) milk
2 cups (500ml) buttermilk
2 tablespoons olive oil
2 eggs, beaten lightly
1⅓ cups (165g) finely grated
    cheddar cheese
⅓ cup (65g) finely chopped,
    bottled jalapeño chillies

1 Place beans in medium bowl, cover with water, stand overnight; drain.

2 Combine beef with the water in large saucepan; bring to a boil; simmer, covered, 1½ hours, cool slightly.

3 Drain beef in large muslin-lined strainer placed over bowl; reserve 3½ cups (875ml) of the cooking liquid. Using two forks, shred beef.

4 Heat oil in same pan; cook brown onion and garlic, stirring, until onion is soft. Add spices; cook, stirring, until fragrant. Add beans, undrained crushed tomatoes, paste and 2 cups (500ml) of the reserved cooking liquid; bring to a boil. Simmer, covered, 1 hour.

5 Add beef and remaining reserved cooking liquid to pan; simmer, covered, about 30 minutes or until beans are tender.

6 Just before serving, stir in green onion, coriander and chilli. Serve chilli con carne with jalapeño corn muffins.

jalapeño corn muffins Preheat oven to moderate. Sift flour and baking powder into large bowl; add remaining ingredients, mix until just combined. Spoon corn muffin mixture into 12-hole (½ cup/125ml) muffin pan. Bake, uncovered, in moderate oven 35 minutes.

serves 8

per serving chilli con carne 11.7g fat; 1292kJ (309 cal)

per muffin 16.7g fat; 1714kJ (410 cal)
serving suggestion Corn chips and guacamole are good served beforehand.
tips If you can find fresh jalapeño chillies, use two, seeded and finely chopped, in both the chilli con carne and the muffins.

massaman beef curry

THAILAND

PREPARATION TIME 25 MINUTES
COOKING TIME 1 HOUR 10 MINUTES (plus cooling time)

¼ cup (60ml) peanut oil
1kg beef topside steak, cut into 3cm cubes
4 small potatoes (480g), halved
3 small brown onions (240g), halved
3¼ cups (810ml) coconut cream
1 teaspoon thick tamarind concentrate
⅔ cup (160ml) hot water
¼ cup (50g) brown sugar

MASSAMAN CURRY PASTE
3 green onions, chopped coarsely
2 cloves garlic, quartered
2 tablespoons chopped fresh lemon grass
2 fresh red thai chillies, chopped coarsely
1 tablespoon coriander seeds
1 tablespoon cumin seeds
3 cardamom pods
½ teaspoon ground nutmeg
¼ teaspoon ground cloves
¼ teaspoon black peppercorns
2 teaspoons shrimp paste
¼ cup (60ml) warm water

1 Heat oil in large saucepan; cook beef, stirring, over high heat until beef is browned all over. Remove beef from pan; drain on absorbent paper.

2 Cook potato and onion in pan; stir over high heat until browned lightly. Stir in massaman curry paste; stir over heat 1 minute.

3 Stir in coconut cream, then stir in beef and combined tamarind concentrate, water and sugar; bring to a boil. Reduce heat, simmer, uncovered, about 45 minutes or until beef is tender and mixture is thickened.

massaman curry paste Preheat oven to moderate. Combine onion, garlic, lemon grass, chilli, seeds, cardamom, nutmeg, clove and peppercorns in small bowl; sprinkle onto oven tray. Bake in moderate oven 10 minutes; cool. Blend or process shrimp paste and the water until combined. Gradually add spice mixture; blend or process until chopped finely.

serves 6

per serving 42.6g fat; 2742kJ (656 cal)
tip This curry can be made two days ahead; store, covered, in the refrigerator. It can also be frozen for up to two months. The paste can be made a week ahead; store, covered, in the refrigerator.

lasagne with beef and spinach   ITALY

PREPARATION TIME **1 HOUR**   COOKING TIME **1 HOUR 30 MINUTES** (plus cooling and standing time)

6 fresh lasagne sheets
1 cup (125g) grated cheddar cheese
½ cup (40g) grated parmesan cheese

CHEESE SAUCE

60g butter
⅓ cup (50g) plain flour
pinch ground nutmeg
2 cups (500ml) milk
1 cup (125g) grated cheddar cheese
¼ cup (20g) grated parmesan cheese

MEAT SAUCE

2 x 400g cans tomatoes
500g beef mince
1 medium brown onion (150g),
  chopped finely
1 clove garlic, crushed
125g button mushrooms, sliced thinly
2 teaspoons chopped fresh oregano
1 teaspoon sugar
⅓ cup (95g) tomato paste

SPINACH LAYER

300g spinach, trimmed,
  shredded coarsely
¼ teaspoon ground nutmeg
½ cup (40g) grated parmesan cheese
250g ricotta cheese
1 egg, beaten lightly

1 Preheat oven to moderate. Spread a quarter of the cheese sauce over base of 20cm x 30cm lamington pan. Place two sheets of pasta over sauce; trim if necessary.

2 Spread half of the meat sauce over pasta; cover with a quarter of the cheese sauce.

3 Spread spinach layer over cheese sauce; top with two more pieces of pasta. Spread with remaining meat sauce and cheese sauce; top with remaining pasta.

4 Sprinkle top with combined cheeses; bake in moderate oven about 40 minutes or until top is golden brown. Remove from oven; let stand 10 minutes before serving.

cheese sauce Melt butter in small saucepan; cook flour and nutmeg, stirring until smooth. Stir over heat 1 minute; gradually add milk. Stir until sauce boils and thickens; reduce heat. Cook 1 minute; remove from heat. Stir in cheeses, stirring until cheese melts.

meat sauce Push tomatoes with their liquid through sieve. Cook mince in large saucepan; stir until meat is browned all over. Add onion, garlic and mushrooms; cook until onion is soft. Add oregano, sugar, tomatoes and paste; bring to a boil. Reduce heat; simmer, covered, 30 minutes. Uncover; simmer about 15 minutes or until sauce is thick.

spinach layer Cook spinach in heated oiled large frying pan until just tender. Press as much liquid as possible from spinach; cool. Combine spinach, nutmeg, cheeses and egg in medium bowl.

serves 6

per serving 37g fat; 2416kJ (578 cal)

osso buco   ITALY

PREPARATION TIME **30 MINUTES**   COOKING TIME **2 HOURS**

The name of this Italian dish translates as "hollow bones". Osso buco is served throughout Italy but is a specialty of Milan.

90g butter
2 medium carrots (240g),
chopped finely
2 large brown onions (400g),
chopped finely
3 trimmed sticks celery (225g),
chopped finely
2 cloves garlic, crushed
16 pieces veal shin or osso buco (2kg)
plain flour
2 tablespoons olive oil
2 x 400g cans tomatoes
½ cup (125ml) dry red wine
1¾ cups (430ml) beef stock
1 tablespoon chopped fresh basil
1 teaspoon chopped fresh thyme
1 bay leaf
2.5cm strip lemon rind
¼ cup chopped fresh flat-leaf parsley
1 teaspoon grated lemon rind

1 Heat a third of the butter in large saucepan; cook carrot, onion, celery and half of the garlic until onion is lightly browned. Remove from heat; transfer vegetables to large ovenproof dish.

2 Coat veal with flour; shake away excess flour. Heat remaining butter and oil in same pan. Add veal; brown well on all sides. Carefully pack veal on top of vegetables. Preheat oven to moderate.

3 Drain fat from pan. Add undrained crushed tomatoes, wine, stock, basil, thyme, bay leaf and strip of lemon rind to same pan; bring sauce to a boil.

4 Pour sauce over veal. Cover casserole; bake in moderate oven about 1½ hours or until veal is very tender, stirring occasionally. To serve, sprinkle with combined remaining garlic, parsley and grated lemon rind.

serves 6

per serving 20.5g fat; 1396kJ (334 cal)
serving suggestion The traditional accompaniment to osso buco is risotto milanese.

teriyaki beef

JAPAN

PREPARATION TIME **10 MINUTES** COOKING TIME **20 MINUTES**

One of the most popular Japanese grilled meat dishes, teriyaki is so easy to prepare at home. Here, we accompany it with fresh baby corn, but try it with grilled red capsicum strips or trimmed sugar snap peas, if you prefer.

½ cup (125ml) mirin
⅓ cup (80ml) light soy sauce
¼ cup (50g) firmly packed brown sugar
1 tablespoon sake
1 tablespoon grated fresh ginger
1 clove garlic, crushed
1 teaspoon sesame oil
1 tablespoon sesame seeds
750g beef fillet, sliced thinly
300g fresh baby corn, halved
2 green onions, sliced thinly

1 Combine mirin, sauce, sugar, sake, ginger, garlic, oil and seeds in large bowl. Stir in beef and corn; stand 5 minutes.

2 Drain beef mixture over medium saucepan; reserve marinade.

3 Cook beef and corn, in batches, on heated oiled grill plate (or grill or barbecue) until browned all over and cooked as desired.

4 Meanwhile, bring marinade to a boil. Reduce heat; simmer, uncovered, 5 minutes.

5 Serve beef and corn drizzled with hot marinade; sprinkle with onion.

serves 4

per serving 12.7g fat; 1818kJ (435 cal)
serving suggestion Serve with boiled or stir-fried noodles.
tip You can substitute pork, fish or chicken for the beef, if you prefer.

beef, tomato and pea pies AUSTRALIA

PREPARATION TIME 15 MINUTES (plus refrigeration time) COOKING TIME 45 MINUTES (plus cooling time)

1 tablespoon vegetable oil
1 small brown onion (80g),
    chopped finely
300g beef mince
400g can tomatoes
1 tablespoon tomato paste
2 tablespoons
    worcestershire sauce
½ cup (125ml) beef stock
½ cup (60g) frozen peas
3 sheets ready-rolled
    puff pastry
1 egg, beaten lightly

1 Heat oil in large saucepan; cook onion, stirring, until softened. Add beef; cook, stirring, until changed in colour. Stir in undrained crushed tomatoes, paste, sauce and stock; bring to a boil. Reduce heat; simmer, uncovered, about 20 minutes or until sauce thickens. Stir in peas. Cool.

2 Preheat oven to moderately hot. Oil six-hole (¾ cup/180ml) Texas muffin pan.

3 Cut two 13cm rounds from opposite corners of each pastry sheet; cut two 9cm rounds from remaining corners of each sheet. Place the six large rounds in muffin pan holes to cover bases and sides; trim any excess pastry. Lightly prick bases with fork; refrigerate 30 minutes. Cover the six small rounds with a damp cloth.

4 Cover pastry-lined muffin pan holes with baking paper; fill holes with uncooked rice or dried beans. Bake, uncovered, in moderately hot oven, 10 minutes; remove paper and rice. Cool.

5 Spoon mince filling into holes; brush edges with a little egg. Top pies with small pastry rounds; gently press around edges to seal.

6 Brush pies with remaining egg; bake, uncovered, in moderately hot oven about 15 minutes or until browned lightly. Stand 5 minutes in pan before serving with mashed potato, if desired.

makes 6

per serving 14g fat; 961kJ (230 cal)

meatloaf with caramelised onion   USA

PREPARATION TIME 25 MINUTES   COOKING TIME 1 HOUR

2 medium brown onions (300g),
  chopped coarsely
2 large carrots (360g),
  chopped coarsely
2 trimmed celery sticks (150g),
  chopped coarsely
2 cloves garlic, quartered
2 cups (200g) packaged breadcrumbs
1 teaspoon salt
1 tablespoon mustard powder
1.5kg beef mince
3 eggs, beaten lightly
2 tablespoons mild chilli sauce
¼ cup (60ml) barbecue sauce
1 cup (250ml) tomato sauce
40g butter
6 medium brown onions (900g),
  sliced thinly, extra
⅓ cup (75g) firmly packed brown sugar
⅓ cup (80ml) cider vinegar

1 Preheat oven to moderate.

2 Blend or process onion, carrot, celery and garlic until chopped finely; place in large bowl. Add breadcrumbs, salt, mustard powder, beef, egg and half of each sauce; using hands, mix until well combined.

3 Divide mixture in half; place each half on lightly oiled swiss roll pan, form each half into a 10cm x 30cm loaf shape.

4 Brush top of meatloaves with half of the remaining combined sauces. Bake in moderate oven, uncovered, brushing meatloaf tops occasionally with remaining combined sauces, about 1 hour or until cooked through.

5 Meanwhile, melt butter in large heavy-based saucepan; cook extra onion, stirring, about 10 minutes or until onion is soft and browned lightly. Stir in sugar and vinegar; cook, stirring, about 15 minutes or until onion is caramelised.

serves 8

per serving 18.7g fat; 2337kJ (559 cal)
serving suggestion Serve with a mixed green salad.
tip Leftover cold meatloaf is great as a sandwich filling, with wholegrain mustard and lettuce.

veal goulash

HUNGARY

PREPARATION TIME **25 MINUTES**
COOKING TIME **1 HOUR 30 MINUTES**

1kg forequarter veal, chopped coarsely
1 tablespoon sweet paprika
2 tablespoons plain flour
2 teaspoons caraway seeds
1 tablespoon vegetable oil
20g butter
1 medium brown onion (150g), chopped finely
1 cup (250ml) beef stock
2 x 400g cans tomatoes
1 tablespoon tomato paste
3 medium potatoes (600g), chopped coarsely
2 teaspoons chopped fresh oregano

1 Toss veal in combined paprika, flour and seeds; shake away excess flour mixture.

2 Heat oil and butter in large saucepan; cook veal, in batches, stirring, until browned. Add onion to pan; cook, stirring, until soft.

3 Return veal to pan with stock, undrained crushed tomatoes and paste; simmer, covered, 30 minutes. Add potato; simmer, covered, about 30 minutes or until veal and potato are tender.

4 Remove cover; simmer about 5 minutes or until thickened slightly. Stir in oregano.

serves 6

per serving 13.5g fat; 1430kJ (342 cal)

tip The goulash can be made a day ahead and stored, covered, in the refrigerator; it is also suitable to freeze.

pastitsio GREECE

PREPARATION TIME 30 MINUTES (plus standing time) COOKING TIME 1 HOUR 45 MINUTES (plus cooling time)

250g macaroni
2 eggs, beaten lightly
¾ cup (60g) grated parmesan cheese
2 tablespoons stale breadcrumbs

MEAT SAUCE
2 tablespoons olive oil
2 medium brown onions (300g),
   chopped finely
750g beef mince
400g can tomatoes
⅓ cup (95g) tomato paste
½ cup (125ml) beef stock
¼ cup (60ml) dry white wine
½ teaspoon ground cinnamon
1 egg, beaten lightly

TOPPING
90g butter
½ cup (75g) plain flour
3½ cups (875ml) milk
1 cup (80g) grated parmesan cheese
2 egg yolks

1 Preheat oven to moderate. Grease shallow 2.5-litre (10 cup) ovenproof dish. Add pasta to large saucepan of boiling water; boil, uncovered, until just tender, drain. Combine hot pasta, egg and cheese in bowl; mix well. Press pasta over base of prepared dish.

2 Top pasta evenly with meat sauce; pour over topping, smooth surface then sprinkle with breadcrumbs. Bake, uncovered, in moderate oven about 1 hour or until lightly browned. Stand 10 minutes before serving.

meat sauce Heat oil in large saucepan, add onion and beef; cook, stirring, until beef is well browned. Stir in undrained crushed tomatoes, paste, stock, wine and cinnamon; simmer, uncovered, until thick. Cool; stir in egg.

topping Melt butter in medium saucepan, add flour; stir over heat until bubbling. Remove from heat; gradually stir in milk. Stir over heat until sauce boils and thickens; stir in cheese, cool slightly. Stir in egg yolks.

serves 6

per serving 51g fat; 3662kJ (876 cal)
serving suggestion Serve with a salad of leafy greens and tomatoes.
tip Pastitsio can be made a day ahead and stored, covered, in the refrigerator; it is also suitable to freeze.

veal parmigiana   ITALY

PREPARATION TIME **35 MINUTES**   COOKING TIME **1 HOUR 20 MINUTES**

4 veal steaks (320g)
plain flour
1 egg
1 tablespoon water
⅓ cup (35g) packaged breadcrumbs
30g butter
⅓ cup (80ml) olive oil
2½ cups (250g) grated
   mozzarella cheese
¾ cup (60g) grated parmesan cheese

TOMATO SAUCE
1 tablespoon olive oil
1 medium brown onion (150g),
   chopped finely
1 trimmed stick celery (75g),
   chopped finely
1 medium red capsicum (200g),
   chopped finely
1 clove garlic, crushed
400g can tomatoes
2 teaspoons sugar
1 tablespoon tomato paste
1½ cups (375ml) chicken stock
1 tablespoon chopped fresh
   flat-leaf parsley
1 tablespoon chopped fresh basil

1 Pound veal out thinly. Toss veal in flour; shake off excess. Dip in combined beaten egg and water; press on breadcrumbs. Refrigerate veal while preparing tomato sauce.

2 Preheat oven to moderate. Heat butter and half of the oil in large frying pan; cook veal until browned on both sides. Place in ovenproof dish; top veal with mozzarella cheese. Spoon tomato sauce over mozzarella cheese.

3 Sprinkle evenly with parmesan cheese; drizzle with remaining oil. Bake, uncovered, in moderate oven about 20 minutes or until golden brown.

tomato sauce   Heat oil in medium frying pan; cook onion, celery, capsicum and garlic, stirring, until onion is soft. Push tomatoes with their liquid through sieve. Add pureed tomato to pan with sugar, paste and stock. Cover; bring to a boil. Reduce heat; simmer, covered, 30 minutes. Remove lid; simmer until sauce is thick. Stir through herbs.

serves 4

per serving 52.8g fat; 3315kJ (793 cal)

spaghetti bolognese
ITALY

PREPARATION TIME 15 MINUTES
COOKING TIME 2 HOURS 15 MINUTES

2 tablespoons olive oil
1 large brown onion (200g), chopped finely
750g beef mince
2 x 400g cans tomatoes
⅓ cup (95g) tomato paste
1 litre (4 cups) water
1 tablespoon shredded fresh basil
1 tablespoon chopped fresh oregano
2 teaspoons chopped fresh thyme
375g spaghetti
⅓ cup (25g) grated parmesan cheese

1 Heat oil in medium frying pan; cook onion until soft.
Add beef to pan; cook until beef is browned all over,
mashing with fork occasionally to break up lumps.

2 Push tomatoes with their liquid through sieve; add to pan.
Add paste and the water; bring to a boil. Reduce heat; cook,
very gently, about 2 hours, uncovered, or until nearly all liquid
is evaporated. Stir in herbs.

3 Meanwhile, cook pasta in large saucepan of boiling water
until tender; drain.

4 Arrange pasta in individual serving bowls; top with sauce.
Sprinkle with cheese.

serves 4

per serving 30g fat; 3248kJ (777 cal)
tip An authentic bolognese sauce contains no garlic, however,
2 crushed cloves of garlic can be added to the onion in step 1,
if desired.

corned beef with parsley sauce   ENGLAND

PREPARATION TIME 20 MINUTES (plus standing time)   COOKING TIME 2 HOURS 15 MINUTES (plus cooling time)

1.5kg whole piece beef
corned silverside
2 bay leaves
6 black peppercorns
1 large brown onion (200g), quartered
1 large carrot (180g), chopped coarsely
1 tablespoon brown malt vinegar
¼ cup (50g) firmly packed brown sugar

PARSLEY SAUCE
30g butter
¼ cup (35g) plain flour
2½ cups (625ml) milk
⅓ cup (40g) grated cheddar cheese
⅓ cup finely chopped fresh
flat-leaf parsley
1 tablespoon mild mustard

1 Combine beef, bay leaves, peppercorns, onion, carrot, vinegar and half of the sugar in large saucepan. Add enough water to just cover beef; simmer, covered, about 2 hours or until beef is tender. Cool beef 1 hour in liquid in pan.

2 Remove beef from pan; discard liquid. Sprinkle sheet of foil with remaining sugar, wrap beef in foil; stand 20 minutes before serving. Serve with parsley sauce.

parsley sauce Melt butter in small saucepan, add flour; cook, stirring, until bubbling. Gradually stir in milk; cook, stirring, until sauce boils and thickens. Remove from heat; stir in cheese, parsley and mustard.

serves 4

per serving 50g fat; 3603kJ (862 cal)

serving suggestion Serve with steamed potatoes and baby carrots, if desired.

boeuf bourguignon FRANCE

PREPARATION TIME **35 MINUTES** COOKING TIME **2 HOURS 30 MINUTES**

If you make your own beef stock, this version of the French classic will be even more flavoursome. Make this casserole a day ahead and store, covered, in the refrigerator to further enrich its full, homely flavour.

1kg beef chuck steak
8 baby onions (200g)
3 bacon rashers (210g)
300g button mushrooms
1 tablespoon olive oil
30g butter
1 clove garlic, crushed
¼ cup (35g) plain flour
1 cup (250ml) beef stock
1 cup (250ml) dry red wine
2 bay leaves
1 tablespoon brown sugar
2 tablespoons chopped fresh oregano

1 Cut away and discard as much fat as possible from beef; cut into 3cm pieces. Peel onions, leaving root end trimmed but intact so onion remains whole during cooking. Cut off and discard rind from bacon; coarsely chop bacon. Trim mushroom stems.

2 Heat oil in large heavy-based flameproof casserole dish; cook beef, in batches, stirring, until browned all over.

3 Heat butter in same dish; cook onions, bacon, mushrooms and garlic over medium-high heat, stirring constantly, until onions are browned all over.

4 Sprinkle flour over onion mixture; cook, stirring, until flour is browned lightly. Remove dish from heat; gradually stir in stock, then wine.

5 Return dish to heat; cook, stirring, until mixture boils and thickens. Return beef with any juices to dish, add bay leaves and sugar; bring to a boil. Simmer, covered, about 2 hours or until beef is tender, stirring every 30 minutes.

6 Discard bay leaves; stir in oregano.

serves 4

per serving 24.5g fat; 2408kJ (576 cal)
serving suggestions Accompany this satisfying dish with fresh crusty bread and a big bowl of greens; alternatively, serve with plain boiled noodles or mashed potatoes.
tips Round, skirt or gravy beef (boned shin) can be used in place of the chuck steak.
The dish you use should have a tight-fitting lid so the casserole's liquid doesn't evaporate, leaving the meat and vegetables scorched.

sukiyaki

JAPAN

PREPARATION TIME **20 MINUTES** COOKING TIME **10 MINUTES**

A traditional sukiyaki pan can be purchased from Japanese stores, however an electric frying pan is a good substitute. Small quantities of sukiyaki are cooked and served individually to guests. Each guest usually has a small bowl containing an egg which has been lightly beaten with chopsticks; the hot food is dipped into the egg before eating. The heat partly cooks the egg.

400g fresh gelatinous noodles (shirataki), drained
8 fresh shiitake mushrooms
600g beef rump steak
4 green onions, sliced thinly
300g spinach, trimmed, chopped coarsely
125g can bamboo shoots, drained
200g firm tofu, cut into 2cm cubes
4 eggs

BROTH
1 cup (250ml) japanese soy sauce
½ cup (125ml) sake
½ cup (125ml) mirin
½ cup (125ml) water
½ cup (110g) caster sugar

1 Rinse noodles under hot water, drain. Cut noodles into 15cm lengths.

2 Remove and discard mushroom stems; cut a cross in the top of caps.

3 Trim beef of all fat; slice thinly. Retain a small piece of beef fat for greasing the sukiyaki pan. Arrange ingredients on platters or in bowls. Place broth in medium bowl. Break eggs into individual bowls; beat lightly.

4 Heat greased sukiyaki pan (or electric frying pan) on a portable gas cooker at the table; add quarter of the beef, stir-fry until partly cooked. Add a quarter of each of the vegetables, tofu, noodles and broth. Dip cooked ingredients in egg before eating.

5 As ingredients and broth are eaten, add remaining ingredients and broth to pan, in batches.

broth Combine ingredients in a medium saucepan; cook over medium heat, stirring, until sugar dissolves.

serves 4

per serving 36.7g fat; 3921kJ (938 cal)
tip You could use beef sirloin or rib eye (scotch fillet) instead of the rump in this recipe.

navarin of lamb

FRANCE

PREPARATION TIME **20 MINUTES** COOKING TIME **1 HOUR 45 MINUTES**

Noisettes are lamb shortloin chops with the bone removed, and the "tail" wrapped around and secured with toothpicks. This dish will improve in flavour if cooked the day before required; store, covered, in the refrigerator.

1 tablespoon olive oil
30g butter
6 lamb noisettes (750g)
1 medium brown onion (150g), chopped coarsely
2 cloves garlic, crushed
⅓ cup (50g) plain flour
1 litre (4 cups) chicken stock
⅓ cup (80ml) dry red wine
2 tablespoons tomato paste
1 large sprig fresh rosemary
2 teaspoons fresh thyme leaves
250g green beans
2 trimmed celery sticks (150g)
250g baby carrots

1 Preheat oven to moderate. Heat oil and butter in large frying pan, add lamb; cook until browned on both sides, remove from pan. Drain all but 2 tablespoons of fat from pan.

2 Add onion and garlic to pan; cook, stirring, until onion is lightly browned. Add flour; stir constantly over heat until mixture is browned. Add stock, wine and paste; stir constantly over heat until mixture boils and thickens. Add herbs; reduce heat, simmer 3 minutes.

3 Meanwhile, cut beans into 5cm lengths. Cut celery into 5cm lengths.

4 Combine lamb, beans, celery and carrots in 2-litre (8 cup) ovenproof dish, top with sauce, cover; bake in moderate oven about 1¼ hours or until lamb is tender.

serves 6

per serving 46.7g fat; 2558kJ (612 cal)

lamb kofta MIDDLE-EAST

PREPARATION TIME **30 MINUTES (plus standing time)** COOKING TIME **15 MINUTES**

½ cup (80g) burghul
1kg lamb mince
1 small brown onion (80g),
  chopped finely
1 teaspoon allspice
1 clove garlic, crushed
1 cup (75g) stale breadcrumbs
1 egg, beaten lightly
¾ cup (200g) yogurt
¼ cup chopped fresh mint

1 Cover burghul with cold water in small bowl; stand 20 minutes or until burghul softens. Drain burghul, squeezing with hands to remove as much water as possible.

2 Using hands, combine burghul with lamb, onion, allspice, garlic, breadcrumbs and egg in large bowl. Divide mixture into 12 balls; mould balls around skewers to form sausage shape. Cook on heated oiled grill plate (or grill or barbecue) until browned all over and cooked through.

3 Serve kofta with combined yogurt and mint and, if desired, hummus (see recipe page 11) and tabbouleh (see recipe page 146).

serves 6

per serving 19.3g fat; 1743kJ (416 cal)
tips Before use, soak bamboo skewers in cold water for at least an hour to prevent them from splintering and scorching.
Lamb can be replaced with minced beef or chicken, if you prefer.

shepherd's pie   ENGLAND

PREPARATION TIME 20 MINUTES   COOKING TIME 45 MINUTES

30g butter

**1 medium brown onion (150g),
    chopped finely**

1 medium carrot (120g), chopped finely

½ teaspoon dried mixed herbs

4 cups (750g) chopped cooked lamb

¼ cup (70g) tomato paste

¼ cup (60ml) tomato sauce

2 tablespoons worcestershire sauce

2 cups (500ml) beef stock

2 tablespoons plain flour

⅓ cup (80ml) water

POTATO TOPPING

5 medium potatoes (1kg), chopped

60g butter, chopped

¼ cup (60ml) milk

1 Preheat oven to moderately hot. Oil shallow 2.5-litre (10 cup) ovenproof dish.

2 Heat butter in large saucepan; cook onion and carrot, stirring, until tender. Add mixed herbs and lamb; cook, stirring, 2 minutes. Stir in paste, sauces and stock, then blended flour and water; stir over heat until mixture boils and thickens. Pour mixture into prepared dish.

3 Place heaped tablespoons of potato topping on lamb mixture. Bake, uncovered, in moderately hot oven about 20 minutes or until browned lightly and heated through.

potato topping   Boil, steam or microwave potatoes until tender; drain. Mash with butter and milk until smooth.

serves 4

per serving 40.2g fat; 3342kJ (798 cal)

tips   This recipe can be made a day ahead; store, covered, in the refrigerator. Shepherd's pie is also suitable to freeze, without the potato topping.

roasted lamb with lemon potatoes

GREECE

PREPARATION TIME 25 MINUTES (plus marinating time)
COOKING TIME 1 HOUR 50 MINUTES

¼ cup (60ml) olive oil
2 tablespoons grated lemon rind
2 tablespoons lemon juice
2 tablespoons dry white wine
2 teaspoons seasoned pepper
2 tablespoons chopped fresh thyme
2kg leg of lamb
2 cloves garlic, sliced
1 tablespoon fresh rosemary leaves

LEMON POTATOES

12 medium old potatoes (2.4kg)
¼ cup (60ml) olive oil
⅓ cup (80ml) lemon juice
1½ tablespoons grated lemon rind
2 tablespoons chopped fresh rosemary
2 tablespoons chopped fresh thyme
1½ teaspoons cracked black pepper

1 Combine oil, rind, juice, wine, pepper and thyme in medium jug; mix well. Trim excess fat from lamb. Using point of knife, make 12 incisions evenly over top of lamb leg. Place a slice of garlic and some of the rosemary leaves in each incision. Pour oil mixture over lamb, cover; refrigerate, turning lamb occasionally, 3 hours or overnight.

2 Preheat oven to moderately hot. Drain lamb, reserve marinade. Place lamb in large baking dish; bake, uncovered, in moderately hot oven 40 minutes. Add lemon potatoes to baking dish with lamb; bake further 50 minutes, turning occasionally, or until lamb and potatoes are tender.

3 Remove lamb from baking dish, cover, keep warm. Drain juices from dish; reserve juices. Return potatoes to very hot oven, bake further 20 minutes or until potatoes are browned and crisp; remove from dish, cover, keep warm. Heat reserved marinade and reserved juices in dish, bring to a boil; serve with sliced lamb, lemon potatoes and, if desired, steamed green beans.

lemon potatoes Cut potatoes into 3cm pieces, place in bowl, pour over combined remaining ingredients; mix well.

serves 6

per serving 24.9g fat; 2850kJ (681 cal)

raan INDIA

PREPARATION TIME 25 MINUTES (plus refrigeration time) COOKING TIME 1 HOUR 35 MINUTES (plus cooling time)

2 teaspoons coriander seeds
1 teaspoon cumin seeds
8 cardamom pods, bruised
2 cinnamon sticks, crushed
2 star anise
½ teaspoon cracked black pepper
6 cloves
4 cloves garlic, crushed
1 tablespoon grated fresh ginger
2 tablespoons lemon juice
¼ cup (70g) tomato paste
2kg leg of lamb
½ cup (125ml) boiling water
¼ teaspoon saffron threads

1 Combine spices in heated dry pan; cook, stirring, until fragrant, cool.

2 Grind or process spice mixture until crushed.

3 Combine crushed spice mixture, garlic, ginger, juice and paste in small bowl; mix well.

4 Trim fat from lamb then pierce lamb all over with deep cuts. Rub spice mixture over lamb, pressing firmly into cuts. Place lamb in large bowl; cover, refrigerate at least 24 hours.

5 Preheat oven to moderate. Pour combined water and saffron into large baking dish; place lamb on oven rack in dish. Cover with foil; bake in moderate oven about 1 hour or until lamb is tender. Remove and discard foil; bake about 30 minutes or until lamb is well browned.

serves 6

per serving 13.6g fat; 1476kJ (353 cal)

tips Raan can be prepared two days ahead and stored, covered, in the refrigerator; uncooked marinated lamb is also suitable to freeze.

serving suggestion Serve with steamed basmati rice, a mixed green salad and dollops of plain yogurt.

moussaka GREECE

PREPARATION TIME **45 MINUTES (plus standing time)** COOKING TIME **2 HOURS (plus cooling time)**

2 large eggplants (1.2kg)
coarse cooking salt
¼ cup (60ml) olive oil
2 tablespoons olive oil, extra
1 large brown onion (200g),
**   chopped finely**
2 cloves garlic, crushed
1kg lamb mince
400g can tomatoes
2 tablespoons tomato paste
½ cup (125ml) dry red wine
2 tablespoons coarsely chopped
**   fresh flat-leaf parsley**
1 teaspoon sugar
¼ teaspoon ground cinnamon
¼ cup (20g) grated parmesan cheese
½ teaspoon ground nutmeg

CHEESE SAUCE
90g butter
½ cup (75g) plain flour
3 cups (750ml) milk
⅓ cup (25g) grated parmesan cheese
2 eggs, beaten lightly

1 Cut eggplants into 5mm slices; sprinkle with salt, stand 20 minutes. Rinse eggplant under cold water; drain, pat dry with absorbent paper. Place eggplant slices in single layer on lightly greased oven trays. Brush with oil, grill on both sides until lightly browned; drain on absorbent paper.

2 Meanwhile, heat extra oil in large saucepan, add onion and garlic; cook, stirring, until onion is soft. Add lamb; cook, stirring, until lamb is browned. Add undrained crushed tomatoes, paste, wine, parsley, sugar and cinnamon; simmer, covered, 30 minutes.

3 Preheat oven to moderate. Grease 2.5-litre (10 cup) ovenproof dish. Line dish with one-third of the eggplant, top with half of the meat sauce, then half of the remaining eggplant, remaining meat sauce and remaining eggplant.

4 Spread cheese sauce over eggplant; sprinkle with cheese and nutmeg. Bake, uncovered, in moderate oven about 45 minutes or until lightly browned.

cheese sauce Melt butter in large saucepan, stir in flour. Stir over heat until bubbling; remove from heat. Gradually stir in milk; stir over heat until mixture boils and thickens. Remove from heat; stir in cheese, cool slightly. Stir in egg; mix until smooth.

serves 6

per serving 54.3g fat; 3298kJ (788 cal)
tip This recipe can be made a day ahead and stored, covered, in the refrigerator; it is also suitable to freeze.

rogan josh   INDIA

PREPARATION TIME **10 MINUTES**   COOKING TIME **2 HOURS 10 MINUTES**

This curry is quite hot; reduce the number of chillies if you like a mild curry.

2 teaspoons ground cardamom
1 teaspoon ground fennel
2 teaspoons ground cumin
2 teaspoons ground coriander
1.4kg trimmed diced lamb shoulder
¼ cup (60ml) vegetable oil
2 medium brown onions (300g),
**   chopped finely**
2 tablespoons grated fresh ginger
6 fresh red thai chillies, seeded,
**   sliced thinly**
4 cloves garlic, crushed
400g can tomatoes
¼ teaspoon saffron threads
2 bay leaves
2 cinnamon sticks
¼ cup (40g) poppy seeds
1 cup (280g) thick yogurt
2 teaspoons brown sugar
¼ cup fresh coriander leaves

1 Combine ground spices in medium bowl, add lamb; toss to cover lamb in spice mix.

2 Heat half of the oil in large saucepan, add lamb; cook, in batches, until browned all over.

3 Heat remaining oil in same pan, add onion, ginger, chilli and garlic; cook, stirring, until onion is soft. Return lamb to pan with undrained crushed tomatoes, saffron, bay leaves, cinnamon sticks and poppy seeds. Add yogurt, 1 tablespoon at a time, stirring well between each addition.

4 Bring to a boil, then reduce heat to very low; cook, covered, about 1¾ hours or until lamb is very tender. Stir in brown sugar; cook, uncovered, 10 minutes or until thickened.

5 Sprinkle with fresh coriander to serve.

serves 6

per serving 34.8g fat; 2270kJ (543 cal)

tips Adding the yogurt a tablespoon at a time helps prevent it from curdling. Rogan josh can be made three days ahead and stored, covered, in the refrigerator; it is also suitable to freeze.

lamb kebabs MIDDLE-EAST

PREPARATION TIME 30 MINUTES COOKING TIME 15 MINUTES

500g diced lamb
¼ cup (60ml) lemon juice
2 tablespoons olive oil
1 clove garlic, crushed
2 medium tomatoes (300g)
½ cup (80g) seeded black olives
200g fetta cheese
1 tablespoon olive oil, extra
8 pocket pitta
80g baby spinach leaves

1 Combine lamb, juice, oil and garlic in medium bowl.

2 Slice tomatoes thickly. Quarter olives; crumble cheese.

3 Thread lamb onto eight skewers; reserve marinade.

4 Heat extra oil in large frying pan; cook kebabs until browned all over and cooked as desired. Pour marinade over kebabs; cook until marinade boils.

5 Serve kebabs on bread with spinach, tomato, olives and cheese.

serves 4

per serving 31.9g fat; 2834kJ (678 cal)

tip If using bamboo skewers, soak them in cold water for at least an hour before use, to prevent them from scorching or splintering.

braised lamb shanks FRANCE

To "french" lamb cuts means to clean away the excess gristle, fat and meat from the end of a shank, cutlet or rack, in order to expose the bone. Ask your butcher to prepare the meat for you this way.

2 tablespoons olive oil

500g (about 6 sticks) trimmed celery, chopped coarsely

2 medium brown onions (300g), chopped coarsely

2 cloves garlic, crushed

2 medium carrots (240g), chopped coarsely

4 french-trimmed lamb shanks (1kg)

¾ cup (180ml) dry white wine

¼ cup (70g) tomato paste

3 cups (750ml) beef stock

2 tablespoons fresh thyme leaves

1½ cups (375ml) beef stock, extra

1½ cups (300g) couscous

1 Heat half of the oil in large saucepan with a tight-fitting lid; cook celery, onion, garlic and carrot, stirring, until onion is soft. Remove vegetables from pan.

2 Heat remaining oil in same pan; cook lamb, uncovered, until browned all over. Stir in wine, paste, stock and thyme, bring to a boil; simmer, covered, 1 hour. Return vegetables to pan; simmer, covered, about 30 minutes or until lamb is tender.

3 Just before serving, prepare the couscous. Bring extra beef stock to a boil in small saucepan; pour stock over couscous in medium heatproof bowl. Stand couscous, covered, fluffing occasionally with fork, about 5 minutes or until stock is absorbed. Serve couscous with lamb and vegetables.

serves 4

per serving 13.4g fat; 2462kJ (589 cal)

serving suggestion While we've served the shanks with couscous, this homely dish also goes well with a mushroom risotto.

tips You can use shanks that haven't been french-trimmed for this dish if you like, but the servings will be larger and have a higher fat content.

This recipe can be frozen, although the couscous should be freshly made.

roast leg of lamb with gravy   ENGLAND

PREPARATION TIME 10 MINUTES   COOKING TIME 2 HOURS (plus standing time)

1 bunch fresh rosemary
2kg leg of lamb
2 cloves garlic, each cut into 8 slices
¼ cup (60ml) olive oil
40g butter
1 small brown onion (80g),
**   chopped finely**
2 tablespoons plain flour
½ cup (125ml) dry red wine
1½ cups (375ml) lamb or beef stock

1 Preheat oven to hot.

2 Cut 16 similar-sized rosemary sprigs from bunch; place remainder of bunch in large flameproof baking dish.

3 Remove and discard as much excess fat from lamb as possible. Pierce surface of lamb all over, making 16 small cuts with a sharp knife; press garlic slices and rosemary sprigs into cuts.

4 Place lamb on oven rack over rosemary in baking dish. Pour oil over the lamb; roast, uncovered, in hot oven 20 minutes. Reduce oven temperature to moderate; roast lamb for 1½ hours. Remove lamb from pan; stand 10 minutes before slicing.

5 Drain juices from pan, melt butter in pan over low heat; cook onion, stirring, until soft. Stir in flour; cook, stirring, about 5 minutes or until browned. Pour in wine and stock; cook over high heat, stirring, until gravy boils and thickens. Strain gravy; serve with lamb and, if desired, roasted vegetables.

serves 6

per serving 26.3g fat; 2082kJ (498 cal)
tips Try substituting fresh lemon thyme, mint or flat-leaf parsley for the rosemary.
Rest the roast, covered in foil, 10 minutes before carving so that the juices '"settle".
When carving the roast, slice across the grain – the meat is more tender this way.

mainspork

spicy pork ribs
CHINA

PREPARATION TIME **10 MINUTES** COOKING TIME **20 MINUTES**

Ask your butcher to cut the pork ribs "American-style" so that as much fat as possible has been removed, leaving only tender, flavoursome meat.

1.5kg trimmed pork spare rib slabs
¾ cup (180ml) light soy sauce
1 egg, beaten lightly
¼ cup (35g) plain flour
2 tablespoons peanut oil
½ cup (125ml) rice wine
½ cup (100g) firmly packed brown sugar
¼ cup yellow mustard seeds
⅓ cup chopped fresh coriander
3 cloves garlic, crushed
1 tablespoon grated fresh ginger
3 teaspoons dried chilli flakes
1 teaspoon five-spice powder
½ teaspoon cayenne pepper

1 Cut pork slabs into individual-rib pieces.

2 Place ribs in large saucepan. Cover with water; bring to a boil. Reduce heat; simmer, uncovered, about 10 minutes or until ribs are almost cooked through. Drain; pat dry with absorbent paper.

3 Blend ¼ cup (60ml) of the sauce, egg and flour in large bowl. Add ribs; stir to coat in soy mixture.

4 Heat oil in wok or large frying pan; stir-fry ribs, in batches, until browned all over.

5 Add remaining ingredients to wok; cook, stirring, until sugar dissolves. Return ribs to wok; stir-fry until heated through.

serves 4

per serving 17.7g fat; 2065kJ (494 cal)
serving suggestion Serve with steamed rice, and individual finger bowls filled with water and a few slices of lemon.
tip Spicy spare ribs can be made a day ahead and stored, covered, in the refrigerator; they can also be frozen for up to 3 months. To serve, reheat in the microwave oven or wok.

sang choy bow CHINA

PREPARATION TIME 15 MINUTES COOKING TIME 15 MINUTES

Packages of already-fried wheat noodles are available from major supermarkets in both spaghetti and fettuccine widths – we used the thinner variety here.

1 tablespoon peanut oil

750g pork mince

2 cloves garlic, crushed

225g can water chestnuts, drained, chopped finely

1 teaspoon sambal oelek

1 tablespoon lime juice

1 medium red capsicum (200g), chopped finely

1 trimmed stick celery (75g), chopped finely

2 tablespoons light soy sauce

2 tablespoons rice vinegar

100g packet fried crunchy noodles

8 large iceberg lettuce leaves

2 green onions, sliced thinly

1 Heat oil in wok or large frying pan; stir-fry pork and garlic until pork changes colour and is cooked through.

2 Stir in water chestnuts, sambal, juice, capsicum, celery, sauce and vinegar; cook, stirring, until vegetables are just tender. Remove from heat; stir in noodles.

3 To serve, divide pork mixture among lettuce leaves; sprinkle each with onion.

serves 4

per serving 21.3g fat 1697kJ (406 cal)

tip The pork mixture, without the noodles, can be made a day ahead; store, covered, in the refrigerator. Add noodles just before serving so they retain their crunch.

cabbage rolls

HUNGARY

PREPARATION TIME **30 MINUTES**
COOKING TIME **1 HOUR 20 MINUTES**

You need 16 large cabbage leaves
for this recipe.

1 medium savoy cabbage (1.5kg)
1 tablespoon olive oil
2 medium brown onions (300g),
    chopped finely
2 cloves garlic, crushed
4 trimmed celery sticks (300g),
    chopped finely
2 bacon rashers (140g),
    chopped finely
700g pork mince
1 cup (200g) long-grain white rice
⅓ cup (95g) tomato paste
400g can tomatoes
3 cups (750ml) chicken stock
2 bay leaves

1 Using a sharp knife, remove core from
bottom of cabbage. Add whole cabbage
to large saucepan of boiling water; cook,
uncovered, about 7 minutes, turning
occasionally, or until leaves just soften.
Place cabbage, bottom-side down, in
colander, drain. Carefully pull off 16 large
leaves without tearing; trim and discard
the hard centre ribs from each leaf. Place
leaves flat on absorbent paper to dry.

2 Heat oil in large saucepan; cook onion
and garlic, stirring, until onion is soft.
Add celery and bacon; cook, stirring,
until celery is tender and bacon cooked
through. Add pork; cook, stirring, until
browned. Remove from heat; stir in
rice and 1 tablespoon of the paste.

3 Place ⅓ cup of the pork mixture in
centre of each cabbage leaf, vein-side
up; fold in sides, roll to enclose filling.

4 Preheat oven to moderate. Combine
undrained crushed tomatoes, remaining
paste, stock and bay leaves in large bowl.

5 Place rolls, seam-side down, in single
layer in large baking dish. Pour tomato
mixture over rolls; cook, covered, in
moderate oven about 1 hour or until rice
is tender and rolls cooked through.
Discard bay leaves before serving.

serves 8

per serving 10g fat; 1321kJ (316 cal)
serving suggestion Top cabbage rolls
with a tablespoon of sour cream, a sprinkle
of sweet paprika and snow pea tendrils;
accompany with fresh crusty bread.

pad thai

THAILAND

PREPARATION TIME **15 MINUTES (plus standing time)** COOKING TIME **15 MINUTES**

This traditional Thai noodle dish is delicious as an accompaniment or as a complete meal. Rice noodles come in varying thicknesses, from very thin strands to flat, wide versions. In Thailand, they usually use sen lek – 5mm-wide rice noodles sometimes called rice stick noodles – for this dish.

12 medium cooked prawns (300g)
250g dried rice noodles
¼ cup (65g) finely chopped palm sugar
1 tablespoon lime juice
1 tablespoon light soy sauce
1 tablespoon tomato sauce
2 tablespoons mild chilli sauce
2 tablespoons fish sauce
2 teaspoons peanut oil
220g chicken mince
200g pork mince
1 clove garlic, crushed
1 tablespoon grated fresh ginger
3 eggs, beaten lightly
2 green onions, sliced thinly
1 cup (80g) bean sprouts
½ cup (75g) roasted unsalted peanuts, chopped coarsely
⅓ cup chopped fresh coriander

1 Shell and devein prawns, leaving tails intact.

2 Place noodles in large heatproof bowl; cover with boiling water. Stand until just tender; drain. Cover to keep warm.

3 Combine sugar, juice and sauces in small bowl.

4 Heat oil in wok or large frying pan; stir-fry chicken, pork, garlic and ginger until meat is cooked through. Add prawns and egg to wok; gently stir-fry until egg sets. Add noodles, sauce mixture and remaining ingredients; stir-fry gently until hot.

serves 4

per serving 24g fat; 2487kJ (595 cal)
serving suggestion Sprinkle pad thai with extra chopped peanuts to serve. Traditionally, this dish is accompanied with a soup, such as tom yum goong, which is consumed like a beverage throughout the meal.
tip Palm sugar, also sold as jaggery, is a product of the coconut palm. It is available from Asian grocery stores, but you can substitute black or brown sugar if unavailable.

rack of pork with stewed apples and sage   ENGLAND

PREPARATION TIME 25 MINUTES   COOKING TIME 1 HOUR 40 MINUTES

Kipfler are small finger-shaped potatoes. You can use halved desiree or pontiac potatoes, if you prefer.

coarse salt
1.3kg pork rack (6 cutlets)
1.25kg kipfler potatoes
750g pumpkin, chopped coarsely
1 tablespoon olive oil

STEWED APPLES AND SAGE
3 large green apples (600g)
¼ cup (60ml) water
4 fresh sage leaves
1 teaspoon sugar

1 Preheat oven to very hot. Rub salt evenly into rind of pork. Cover bones with foil to prevent burning. Place pork, rind-side up, in large baking dish; bake, uncovered, in very hot oven about 35 minutes or until rind is blistered and browned.

2 Place potatoes and pumpkin in separate baking dish, drizzle with oil. Reduce oven temperature to moderate; bake pork and vegetables, uncovered, about 40 minutes or until pork is cooked through. Remove pork from dish; cover with foil to keep warm.

3 Increase oven temperature to very hot; bake vegetables for 15 minutes or until browned and tender. Serve pork with roasted vegetables, stewed apples and sage and, if desired, steamed green beans.

stewed apples and sage   Peel and core apples; cut into thick slices. Combine apple, the water and sage in medium saucepan; simmer, uncovered, about 10 minutes or until apple is soft. Remove from heat, stir in sugar.

serves 6

per serving   11.4g fat; 1764kJ (422 cal)

nasi goreng   INDONESIA

PREPARATION TIME **10 MINUTES**   COOKING TIME **10 MINUTES**

Nasi goreng is the Indonesian name for fried rice – easily made using leftover white rice. Shrimp paste, also known as trasi and blachan, is available from Asian grocery stores and selected supermarkets. You will need to cook about 1½ cups (300g) long-grain white rice for this recipe.

1 small brown onion (100g),
**   chopped coarsely**
2 cloves garlic, quartered
1 teaspoon shrimp paste
2 tablespoons peanut oil
4 eggs
125g small shelled uncooked prawns
4 cups (600g) cold, cooked
**   long-grain white rice**
3 green onions, sliced thinly
125g chinese barbecued pork,
**   sliced thinly**
2 tablespoons light soy sauce

1 Blend or process brown onion, garlic and paste until almost smooth.

2 Heat half of the oil in medium frying pan, break eggs into pan; cook, uncovered, until egg white has set and yolk is cooked as desired.

3 Meanwhile, heat remaining oil in wok or large frying pan; stir-fry onion mixture until fragrant. Add prawns; stir-fry until prawns just change colour.

4 Add rice, green onion, pork and sauce; stir-fry until hot. Serve nasi goreng with eggs.

serves 4

per serving   19.9g fat; 1927kJ (461 cal)

pork vindaloo

INDIA

PREPARATION TIME **15 MINUTES** (plus refrigeration time)
COOKING TIME **1 HOUR 15 MINUTES** (plus cooling time)

We used pork cut from leg steaks in this traditional Goan recipe.
Portuguese missionaries introduced vinegar to this west Indian state to
help meat keep longer and to add a sensational tang to a fiery curry.

2 teaspoons cumin seeds
2 teaspoons garam masala
1 tablespoon grated fresh ginger
6 cloves garlic, crushed
8 fresh red thai chillies, chopped finely
1 tablespoon white vinegar
1 tablespoon tamarind concentrate
1kg diced pork
2 tablespoons ghee
2 large brown onions (400g), chopped coarsely
2 cinnamon sticks
6 cloves
2 teaspoons plain flour
1 litre (4 cups) beef stock
8 curry leaves
2 tablespoons finely chopped palm sugar

1 Cook cumin and garam masala in large heated dry saucepan,
stirring until fragrant; cool.

2 Combine cumin mixture with ginger, garlic, chilli, vinegar, tamarind
and pork in large bowl; cover, refrigerate 1 hour.

3 Heat ghee in same pan; cook onion, cinnamon and cloves, stirring,
until onion is browned lightly. Add pork mixture; cook, stirring, about
5 minutes or until pork is browned lightly. Stir in flour.

4 Add stock gradually, stir in leaves; simmer, covered, 30 minutes.
Remove cover; simmer about 30 minutes or until pork is tender
and sauce thickened. Add palm sugar; stir until dissolved.

serves 6

per serving 30.7g fat; 2048kJ (490 cal)
serving suggestion Serve pork vindaloo with steamed basmati rice.
tip The vindaloo can be made a day ahead; store, covered,
in the refrigerator.

mainsseafood

honey prawns
CHINA

PREPARATION TIME 30 MINUTES COOKING TIME 15 MINUTES

1.5kg large uncooked prawns
1 cup (150g) self-raising flour
1¼ cups (310ml) water
1 egg, beaten lightly
cornflour
vegetable oil, for deep-frying
2 teaspoons peanut oil
¼ cup (90g) honey
100g snow pea sprouts
2 tablespoons sesame seeds, toasted

1 Shell and devein prawns, leaving tails intact. Sift self-raising flour into medium bowl; gradually whisk in the water and egg until batter is smooth. Just before serving, coat prawns in cornflour, shake off excess; dip into batter, one at a time, draining away excess.

2 Heat vegetable oil in wok or large frying pan; deep-fry prawns, in batches, until browned lightly. Drain on absorbent paper.

3 Heat peanut oil in same cleaned wok or large frying pan; heat honey, uncovered, until bubbling. Add prawns; coat with honey mixture. Serve prawns on snow pea sprouts, sprinkled with seeds.

serves 4

per serving 26.7g fat; 2654kJ (635 cal)

fish cakes   THAILAND

PREPARATION TIME **30 MINUTES (plus refrigeration time)** COOKING TIME **20 MINUTES**

We recommend using redfish or flathead fillets for this recipe.

1kg boneless skinless fish fillets
3 green onions, chopped finely
2 cloves garlic, crushed
¼ cup chopped fresh coriander
2 tablespoons red curry paste
1 egg
¼ cup (60ml) coconut milk
100g green beans, sliced thinly
peanut oil, for shallow-frying

1 Blend or process fish, onion, garlic, coriander, paste, egg and coconut milk until just combined. Stir beans into mixture.

2 Using hands, shape level tablespoons of fish mixture into cakes, place on tray, cover; refrigerate 30 minutes.

3 Heat oil in large frying pan; shallow-fry fish cakes, in batches, about 3 minutes or until lightly browned both sides and cooked through (do not overcook or fish cakes will become rubbery). Drain on absorbent paper. If desired, serve fish cakes with separate dipping bowls of combined soy sauce, sweet chilli sauce and green onion, as well as steamed jasmine rice and a mixed green salad.

makes 56

per fish cake 3.8g fat; 782kJ (187 cal)
tip Uncooked fish cakes can be prepared a day ahead; store, covered, in the refrigerator.

salt and pepper squid CHINA

PREPARATION TIME **15 MINUTES** COOKING TIME **5 MINUTES**

In China, this dish is usually enjoyed as a starter but, when you add boiled rice and wilted Asian greens, it makes a substantial main meal.

500g squid hoods
¾ cup (110g) plain flour
1 tablespoon salt
2 tablespoons ground black pepper
vegetable oil, for deep-frying
150g mesclun

CHILLI DRESSING
½ cup (125ml) sweet chilli sauce
1 teaspoon fish sauce
¼ cup (60ml) lime juice
1 clove garlic, crushed

1 Cut squid in half lengthways; score inside surface of each piece. Cut into 2cm-wide strips.

2 Combine flour, salt and pepper in large bowl; add squid. Coat in flour mixture; shake off excess.

3 Heat oil in wok or large saucepan; deep-fry squid, in batches, until tender and browned all over, drain on absorbent paper.

4 Serve squid on mesclun with chilli dressing.

chilli dressing Combine ingredients in screw-top jar; shake well.

serves 4

per serving 12.2g fat; 1375kJ (329 cal)
serving suggestion Serve with wedges of lime or lemon for added piquancy.
tip Place flour, salt and pepper in a strong plastic bag with squid; hold the bag tightly closed, then gently shake to coat the squid in flour mixture. Remove squid from bag, shaking off any excess flour.

spaghetti alla vongole
ITALY

PREPARATION TIME 30 MINUTES (plus soaking time)
COOKING TIME 40 MINUTES

1.5kg clams
1 tablespoon coarse cooking salt
¼ cup (60ml) olive oil
1 medium brown onion (150g), chopped finely
2 cloves garlic, crushed
2 anchovy fillets, drained, chopped finely
1 fresh red thai chilli, seeded, chopped finely
2 teaspoons chopped fresh thyme
20 medium egg tomatoes (1.5kg), peeled,
**   seeded, chopped finely**
2 tablespoons chopped fresh flat-leaf parsley
500g spaghetti

1 Rinse clams under cold water and place in large bowl. Sprinkle with salt, cover with cold water and soak for 2 hours (this purges them of any grit). Discard water, then rinse clams thoroughly; drain.

2 Heat 2 tablespoons of the oil in large saucepan, add clams, cover with tight-fitting lid. Cook over high heat about 8 minutes or until all clams have opened.

3 Strain clam cooking liquid through fine cloth or tea-towel. Return liquid to clean pan; cook, uncovered, until liquid is reduced to 1 cup (250ml). Reserve clam stock.

4 Heat remaining oil in another saucepan, add onion, garlic, anchovy, chilli and thyme; cook, stirring, until onion is soft. Add tomato and reserved clam stock; cook, uncovered, about 10 minutes or until sauce is thickened. Add clams, stir until heated through. Stir in parsley.

5 Meanwhile, add pasta to large saucepan of boiling water; boil, uncovered, until just tender, drain. Toss clam sauce through spaghetti.

serves 6

per serving 11g fat; 1877kJ (449 cal)

fish and chips   ENGLAND

PREPARATION TIME **30 MINUTES (plus refrigeration time)**   COOKING TIME **30 MINUTES**

1½ cups (225g) self-raising flour
1 egg
1½ cups (375ml) beer
5 large potatoes (1.5kg)
vegetable oil, for deep-frying
12 flathead fillets (660g)

TARTARE SAUCE
1 cup (300g) mayonnaise
2 teaspoons finely grated lemon rind
1 tablespoon lemon juice
2 tablespoons finely chopped gherkins
2 tablespoons drained capers,
  chopped finely
1 tablespoon finely chopped fresh dill
1 tablespoon finely chopped
  fresh chives
1 fresh red thai chilli, seeded,
  chopped finely

1 Whisk flour, egg and beer together in medium bowl until smooth, cover; refrigerate 1 hour.

2 Meanwhile, preheat oven to moderate. Cut peeled potatoes into 1cm-wide slices; cut slices into 1cm-wide strips. Pat potato chips completely dry with absorbent paper.

3 Heat oil in large saucepan; deep-fry chips, in batches, until browned and cooked through. Place chips on absorbent paper on large oven tray; place, uncovered, in moderate oven.

4 Reheat oil. Dip fish in beer batter, drain away excess batter. Deep-fry fish, in batches, until browned and crisp.

5 Serve fish and chips with tartare sauce and, if desired, lemon wedges.

tartare sauce   Combine ingredients in medium bowl; mix well.

serves 4

per serving   60.7g fat; 4952kJ (1183 cal)
tip   The best varieties of potato to use for chips are bintje, nicola, patrone or russet burbank.

fish milanese ITALY

PREPARATION TIME 20 MINUTES (plus marinating time) COOKING TIME 10 MINUTES

4 fish fillets (800g)

1 small brown onion (80g),
   chopped finely

2 tablespoons lemon juice

⅓ cup (80ml) olive oil

plain flour

2 eggs

1 tablespoon milk

packaged breadcrumbs

1 tablespoon olive oil, extra

120g butter

1 clove garlic, crushed

1 tablespoon chopped fresh
   flat-leaf parsley

1 Remove skin and bones from fish. Combine onion, juice and oil in shallow dish; mix well. Add fish, spoon mixture over fish to coat thoroughly, cover; refrigerate 1 hour, turning occasionally.

2 Remove fish from marinade; coat lightly with flour. Combine eggs and milk in small bowl; beat lightly. Dip fish in egg mixture. Cover fish with breadcrumbs; press breadcrumbs on firmly.

3 Heat extra oil and half of the butter in large frying pan. Cook fish until golden brown and cooked through; drain on absorbent paper.

4 Melt remaining butter in small saucepan. Cook garlic until butter turns light golden brown; add parsley. Pour browned butter over fillets.

serves 4

per serving 52.9g fat; 2926kJ (700 cal)

serving suggestion Serve with leafy salad greens and lemon wedges.

char kway teow

MALAYSIA

PREPARATION TIME **25 MINUTES** COOKING TIME **10 MINUTES**

This classic Malaysian fried noodle dish is best made with fresh noodles.

1kg fresh rice noodles
500g small uncooked prawns
2 tablespoons peanut oil
340g chicken breast fillets, chopped coarsely
4 fresh red thai chillies, seeded, chopped finely
2 cloves garlic, crushed
2 teaspoons grated fresh ginger
5 green onions, sliced thinly
2 cups (160g) bean sprouts
⅓ cup (80ml) soy sauce
¼ teaspoon sesame oil
1 teaspoon brown sugar

1 Place noodles in large heatproof bowl, cover with boiling water; gently separate with fork, drain.

2 Shell and devein prawns, leaving tails intact; halve prawns crossways.

3 Heat half of the peanut oil in wok or large frying pan; stir-fry chicken, chilli, garlic and ginger until chicken is cooked through. Remove from wok.

4 Heat remaining peanut oil in wok; stir-fry prawns until they just change colour. Remove from wok. Stir-fry onion and sprouts in wok until onion is soft. Add noodles and combined remaining ingredients; stir-fry 1 minute.

5 Return chicken mixture and prawns to wok; stir-fry until heated through.

serves 6

per serving 10.4g fat; 1464kJ (350 cal)
tip Char kway teow is best made just before serving.

chilli crab   SINGAPORE

PREPARATION TIME **20 MINUTES**   COOKING TIME **15 MINUTES**

Chilli crab is one of Singapore's signature dishes. There is no elegant way to eat this meal, so have finger bowls and plenty of napkins handy. Nutcrackers make breaking open the claws easier and a long, narrow seafood fork helps remove the flesh.

**8 large uncooked blue
   swimmer crabs (3kg)**
1 tablespoon peanut oil
**4 fresh red thai chillies, seeded,
   chopped finely**
2 tablespoons grated fresh ginger
4 cloves garlic, crushed
1 tablespoon fish sauce
⅓ cup (80ml) tomato sauce
¼ cup (60ml) sweet chilli sauce
2 tablespoons brown sugar
1 cup (250ml) fish stock
1 cup (250ml) water
¼ cup chopped fresh coriander

1 Remove the v-shaped flaps on the undersides of crabs. Turn crabs over and place your fingers (if the crabs are large, you may need to use a knife) in the seam between the back two legs, and push up to lever off the shells. Pull the shells up and remove them.

2 Remove the feathery gills. Cut each crab in half through the centre of the body, then shake out the gut, which is the grey- or mustard-coloured substance; rinse lightly (avoid using too much water for this and don't rinse under a running tap – as doing so will dilute the delicate flavour).

3 Remove the claws from the crabs. Crack both sections of the claws, using a shellfish cracker, a nutcracker or a meat mallet – this allows the spicy sauce to be absorbed and makes it easier to remove the flesh for eating.

4 Heat oil in wok or large pan; cook chilli, ginger and garlic until fragrant. Add combined sauces, then sugar, stock and the water; stir until mixture boils. Transfer two-thirds of the sauce to a jug; reserve. Add claws to sauce remaining in wok; stir-fry about 4 minutes or until claws have changed in colour and are just cooked through. Remove claws from wok; cover to keep warm. Add half of the reserved sauce and half of the crab bodies to the wok; stir-fry 5 minutes or until cooked through, remove. Repeat with remaining sauce and crab bodies. Serve sprinkled with coriander.

serves 4

per serving 7.6g fat; 1442kJ (345 cal)

tip This recipe is best made close to serving. Mud crabs are traditionally used for this recipe, but we've used blue swimmer crabs, as they are readily available and less expensive.

spaghetti marinara   ITALY

PREPARATION TIME 20 MINUTES COOKING TIME 20 MINUTES

500g cooked medium prawns
375g spaghetti
½ cup (125ml) water
½ cup (125ml) dry white wine
250g scallops, halved
2 tablespoons olive oil
5 large tomatoes (1.4kg),
   chopped coarsely
2 cloves garlic, crushed
1 tablespoon tomato paste
8 oysters
45g can anchovy fillets, drained,
   chopped finely
1 tablespoon chopped fresh
   flat-leaf parsley
1 tablespoon chopped fresh mint

1 Shell and devein prawns.

2 Cook pasta in large saucepan of boiling water until tender; drain.

3 Meanwhile, combine the water and wine in large saucepan; cook scallops 1 minute. Remove scallops; drain.

4 Heat oil in large frying pan; cook tomato, garlic and paste for 2 minutes. Add seafood to pan; cook 1 minute. Add parsley and mint; stir through. Serve sauce over pasta.

serves 4

per serving 12.6g fat; 2366kJ (566 cal)

smoked fish kedgeree   ENGLAND

PREPARATION TIME **10 MINUTES** COOKING TIME **10 MINUTES**

You will need about 1⅓ cups uncooked rice for this recipe – we used basmati rice.

1 tablespoon olive oil
1 large brown onion (300g),
 sliced thinly
60g butter, chopped
1 clove garlic, crushed
2 teaspoons curry powder
4 green onions, sliced thinly
⅓ cup (40g) frozen peas
4 cups cooked rice
415g can red salmon, drained
2 tablespoons chopped fresh
 flat-leaf parsley
1 tablespoon lemon juice
3 hard-boiled eggs, chopped coarsely

1 Heat oil in large frying pan; cook brown onion, stirring, until soft and browned. Remove from pan, keep warm.

2 Melt butter in same pan; cook garlic, curry powder and green onion, stirring, about 3 minutes or until fragrant.

3 Add peas, rice and salmon; stir until heated through. Stir in parsley and juice. Serve kedgeree topped with egg and brown onion.

serves 4

per serving 31.3g fat; 3504kJ (599 cal)

crab cakes   USA

PREPARATION TIME **30 MINUTES**   COOKING TIME **15 MINUTES**

2 green onions, chopped finely
1 trimmed celery stick (75g),
   chopped finely
500g crab meat
2 egg whites, beaten lightly
1 tablespoon finely chopped fresh dill
1 tablespoon worcestershire sauce
1 cup (70g) stale breadcrumbs

SOY AND HONEY SAUCE
½ cup (125ml) soy sauce
2 tablespoons honey

1   Cook onion and celery in large heated oiled non-stick frying pan until onion is soft.

2   Combine onion mixture with remaining ingredients in large bowl. Using hands, shape mixture into 12 cakes.

3   Cook cakes, in batches, in same pan until browned both sides and cooked through.

4   Serve crab cakes with soy and honey sauce and, if desired, a mixed green salad.

soy and honey sauce   Combine ingredients in small bowl.

serves 4

per serving   1.4g fat; 869kJ (208 cal)

salmon teriyaki   JAPAN

PREPARATION TIME 10 MINUTES (plus marinating and soaking time) COOKING TIME 10 MINUTES

Daikon is a large white radish with a sweet, fresh taste. In Japan it is often served, grated raw, as an accompaniment.

4 salmon fillets (700g), skinned
½ cup (120g) finely shredded daikon

TERIYAKI MARINADE
⅔ cup (160ml) japanese soy sauce
⅔ cup (160ml) mirin
2 tablespoons sake
1 tablespoon sugar

1 Place salmon in teriyaki marinade for 10 minutes, turning occasionally. Drain salmon over medium bowl; reserve marinade.

2 Meanwhile, soak daikon in small bowl of iced water for 15 minutes; drain well.

3 Cook salmon on heated oiled grill plate (or grill or barbecue), brushing occasionally with marinade, until cooked as desired. Bring reserved marinade to a boil in small saucepan. Reduce heat; simmer 5 minutes or until sauce thickens slightly.

4 Serve salmon with daikon, drizzle with sauce.

teriyaki marinade Combine ingredients in medium bowl; stir until sugar dissolves.

serves 4

per serving 15.7g fat; 1417kJ (339 cal)
tip Bought teriyaki sauce may be used, but it's stronger than homemade. Dilute it with mirin, sake or water.

mee goreng   INDONESIA

PREPARATION TIME **15 MINUTES**   COOKING TIME **15 MINUTES**

Mee goreng, from Indonesia, translates simply as fried noodles. There are many different versions of this Asian mainstay – all of them easy to make. This recipe uses prawns, but it's often made with chicken, pork or beef.

500g fresh rice noodles
20 medium uncooked prawns (500g)
1 tablespoon peanut oil
3 eggs, beaten lightly
2 cloves garlic, crushed
2 teaspoons grated fresh ginger
4 trimmed sticks celery (300g),
**   sliced thinly**
4 green onions, sliced thinly
¼ cup chopped fresh coriander
¼ cup (60ml) light soy sauce
½ cup (75g) roasted unsalted peanuts,
**   chopped coarsely**
1 lebanese cucumber (130g), halved
**   lengthways, seeded, sliced thinly**

1 Rinse noodles under hot water; drain. Transfer to large bowl; separate noodles with fork. Shell and devein prawns; cut in half lengthways.

2 Brush heated wok or large frying pan with a little of the oil. Add half of the egg; swirl to cover base of wok. Cook, covered, about 3 minutes or until cooked through. Remove omelette from wok; repeat with remaining egg. Roll omelettes tightly; slice thinly.

3 Heat remaining oil in wok; stir-fry prawns, garlic, ginger and celery until prawns just change colour. Add noodles, onion, coriander and sauce; stir-fry until heated through. Serve immediately sprinkled with omelette, peanuts and cucumber.

serves 4

per serving   18.4g fat; 1676kJ (401 cal)
serving suggestion   You could serve this dish with a small side bowl of either finely sliced red thai chillies or chilli sauce, for those who like it hot.
tip   You can substitute your favourite noodles for the rice noodles. However, you may need to adjust the cooking time.

paella

SPAIN

PREPARATION TIME **20 MINUTES (plus soaking and standing time)**
COOKING TIME **40 MINUTES**

A time-honoured Spanish favourite, paella is a wonderful one-pot dish for
entertaining – or just because it tastes great. The traditional pan for this recipe
is shallow and wide. If you don't have a paella pan or a large enough frying pan,
use two smaller frying pans – the mixture should only be about 4cm deep.
This recipe is best made just before serving.

500g clams
1 tablespoon coarse salt
300g medium uncooked prawns
500g small black mussels
1 pinch saffron threads
¼ cup (60ml) hot water
2 tablespoons olive oil
2 chicken thigh fillets (220g), chopped coarsely
200g chorizo sausage, sliced
1 large red onion (300g), chopped
1 medium red capsicum (200g), chopped
2 cloves garlic, crushed
2 teaspoons sweet paprika
1½ cups (300g) medium-grain white rice
3½ cups (875ml) chicken stock
1 cup (125g) frozen peas
2 medium tomatoes (380g), peeled, seeded, chopped finely

1   Rinse clams under cold water and place in large bowl. Sprinkle with salt,
    cover with cold water and soak for 2 hours (this purges them of any grit).
    Discard water then rinse clams thoroughly; drain. Shell and devein prawns,
    leaving tails intact. Scrub mussels and remove beards. Combine saffron
    and the hot water in small bowl; stand for 30 minutes.

2   Heat oil in a 40cm-wide shallow pan, add chicken; cook until browned.
    Remove chicken. Add chorizo to same pan; cook until browned, drain on
    absorbent paper. Add onion, capsicum, garlic and paprika; cook, stirring,
    until soft. Add rice and stir until it is coated in oil. Return chicken and
    chorizo to pan.

3   Add stock and saffron mixture; stir until combined. Bring to a boil; simmer,
    uncovered, about 12 minutes or until rice is almost tender. Sprinkle peas and
    tomato over rice; simmer, uncovered, 3 minutes.

4   Place clams, mussels and prawns over rice mixture. Cover pan with foil
    and simmer for 5 minutes or until clams and mussels have opened and
    prawns are cooked. Discard any unopened shells.

serves 4

per serving 30g fat; 2926kJ (700 cal)
tips Chorizo is a spicy pork sausage made with garlic and red capsicums.
Saffron threads are available at specialty food stores and some supermarkets.
If unavailable, substitute a tiny pinch of saffron powder.

fish with chermoulla   MIDDLE-EAST

PREPARATION TIME **15 MINUTES**   COOKING TIME **15 MINUTES**

1kg snapper fillet
3 cloves garlic, crushed
1 teaspoon ground cumin
½ teaspoon hot paprika
2 tablespoons coarsely chopped
**   fresh coriander**
2 tablespoons coarsely chopped
**   fresh flat-leaf parsley**
¼ cup (60ml) olive oil
2 teaspoons finely grated lemon rind
¼ cup (60ml) lemon juice

1   Cut fish into eight even-sized pieces. Place in large shallow dish.

2   Combine remaining ingredients in medium bowl. Pour half of the chermoulla over fish.

3   Cook fish, in batches, in heated oiled non-stick frying pan until browned both sides and cooked through.

4   Serve fish drizzled with remaining chermoulla; sprinkle with extra coriander leaves, if desired.

serves 4

per serving   18.7g fat; 1568kJ (375 cal)

salmon with dill and caper dressing   SCANDINAVIA

PREPARATION TIME **10 MINUTES**   COOKING TIME **10 MINUTES**

¼ cup (60g) sour cream
1 tablespoon drained tiny capers
2 teaspoons finely chopped fresh dill
2 teaspoons horseradish cream
1 teaspoon lime juice
4 small salmon fillets (600g)

1 Combine sour cream, capers, dill, horseradish and juice in medium bowl.

2 Cook salmon on heated oiled grill plate (or grill or barbecue) until browned both sides and cooked as desired.

3 Serve salmon with dill and caper dressing.

serves 4

per serving 9.8g fat; 666kJ (159 cal)
serving suggestion Serve salmon with a mixed green salad, steamed baby potatoes and lime wedges.

piri-piri chicken
PORTUGAL

PREPARATION TIME 15 MINUTES (plus marinating time)
COOKING TIME 1 HOUR 15 MINUTES

1.5kg whole chicken
4 fresh red thai chillies, seeded, chopped finely
1 tablespoon sweet paprika
2 teaspoons dried oregano
2 teaspoons salt
1 tablespoon brown sugar
½ cup (125ml) lemon juice
2 tablespoons olive oil

1 Wash chicken under cold water; pat dry with absorbent paper. Using kitchen scissors, cut along both sides of backbone of chicken; discard backbone. Place chicken, skin-side up, on board; using heel of hand, press down on breastbone to flatten chicken. Insert metal skewer through thigh and opposite wing of chicken to keep chicken flat. Repeat with other thigh and wing.

2 Combine remaining ingredients in large bowl, add chicken; spoon marinade all over chicken. Cover; refrigerate 3 hours or overnight.

3 Preheat oven to hot. Drain chicken over same large bowl; reserve marinade. Place chicken on oiled wire rack over baking dish; pour over reserved marinade. Bake, uncovered, in hot oven, brushing occasionally with pan juices, about 1¼ hours or until chicken is browned and cooked through.

serves 4

per serving 39.5g fat; 2203kJ (527 cal)
serving suggestion Serve with a crisp garden salad, lemon wedges and crusty bread.
tip Portuguese chicken can also be grilled on a barbecue or cooked on a pizza stone in the oven.

chicken satay MALAYSIA

PREPARATION TIME 30 MINUTES (plus marinating time) COOKING TIME 15 MINUTES

Soak bamboo skewers in water for a least 1 hour before use to avoid scorching and splintering during cooking.

1kg chicken thigh fillets
¼ cup (60ml) lemon juice
1 teaspoon sambal oelek
1 teaspoon ground turmeric

SATAY SAUCE
¾ cup (195g) peanut butter
1½ cups (375ml) chicken stock
½ cup (125ml) mild sweet chilli sauce
2 tablespoons lemon juice

1 Cut chicken into 2cm pieces. Combine chicken with remaining ingredients in bowl; mix well. Cover, refrigerate several hours or overnight.

2 Thread chicken onto 12 skewers.

3 Cook skewers on heated oiled grill plate (or grill or barbecue) until browned and cooked through. Serve with satay sauce and, if desired, steamed rice.

satay sauce Combine ingredients in medium saucepan; simmer, stirring, about 3 minutes or until thickened.

serves 4

per serving 44.1g fat; 2883kJ (690 cal)
tips The satay sauce can be made a day ahead; store, covered, in the refrigerator.
The marinated uncooked chicken is suitable to freeze.

chicken tikka INDIA

PREPARATION TIME **15 MINUTES (plus marinating time)** COOKING TIME **10 MINUTES**

Chicken and duck are treated with higher regard in the Indian kitchen than in our own. Because they are relatively expensive, they receive special handling, whether with overnight spicing for tandoor cooking, slow simmering with rich sauces or luxuriously strewn with nuts upon serving.

1kg single chicken breast fillets
1 tablespoon grated fresh ginger
3 cloves garlic, crushed
2 tablespoons lemon juice
2 teaspoons ground coriander
2 teaspoons ground cumin
½ teaspoon garam masala
½ teaspoon chilli powder
⅓ cup (95g) yogurt
2 tablespoons tomato paste
pinch tandoori powder

1 Cut chicken fillets in half diagonally; make three shallow cuts across each piece.

2 Combine remaining ingredients in large bowl; add chicken, stir to coat with marinade. Cover, refrigerate overnight.

3 Cook chicken on heated oiled grill plate (or grill or barbecue) until browned and cooked through.

serves 4

per serving 14.7g fat; 1542kJ (369 cal)
serving suggestion Serve with a salad of baby spinach, lemon wedges and steamed rice.

chicken kiev   RUSSIA

This recipe can also be made into chicken cordon bleu. After fillets have been cut in half horizontally almost all the way through, place a piece of swiss cheese and a piece of smoked ham into opening; secure with toothpicks. Continue with crumbing before shallow-frying.

100g butter, softened

3 cloves garlic, crushed

1 teaspoon grated lemon rind

2 tablespoons chopped fresh flat-leaf parsley

2 tablespoons chopped fresh chives

4 single chicken breast fillets (700g)

⅓ cup (50g) plain flour

2 eggs, beaten lightly

2 cups (140g) stale breadcrumbs

vegetable oil, for deep-frying

1 Combine butter, garlic, rind, parsley and chives in small bowl; beat with wooden spoon until combined. Spoon butter mixture onto piece of plastic wrap, shape into 20cm log, wrap tightly; freeze until firm.

2 Cut chicken fillets in half horizontally almost all the way through. Open out each fillet, place between sheets of plastic wrap; gently pound with meat mallet until 1cm thick.

3 Cut butter log into four pieces, place a piece of butter at one end of a chicken piece; roll once, fold in sides, roll up. Toss chicken roll in flour; dip in egg, then roll in crumbs. Repeat with remaining butter and chicken, then flour, egg and crumbs. Refrigerate rolls 30 minutes.

4 Heat oil in medium saucepan to 160°C. Deep-fry chicken, in two batches, about 10 minutes or until well browned and cooked through. Drain well on absorbent paper.

serves 4

per serving   49.9g fat; 3206kJ (767 cal)

serving suggestion   Serve with lemon wedges and steamed asparagus.

yakitori chicken   JAPAN

PREPARATION TIME **15 MINUTES** COOKING TIME **10 MINUTES**

Yakitori is a popular Japanese dish – tiny skewers of grilled chicken pieces, served with a dipping sauce. Sometimes accompanied by mushrooms, capsicum strips, onion wedges or quail eggs, the skewers can be threaded with chicken breast or thigh fillet, chicken liver or even minced chicken gizzards.

1kg chicken breast fillets
¼ cup (60ml) mirin
½ cup (125ml) light soy sauce
2 teaspoons grated fresh ginger
2 cloves garlic, crushed
¼ teaspoon ground black pepper
1 tablespoon sugar

1 Cut chicken into 2cm pieces.

2 Combine chicken with remaining ingredients in large bowl. Drain chicken over small bowl; reserve marinade.

3 Thread chicken onto 12 bamboo skewers. Cook skewers on heated oiled grill plate (or grill or barbecue), turning and brushing with reserved marinade occasionally. Cook until yakitori are browned all over and cooked through.

serves 4

per serving 13.8g fat; 1613kJ (386 cal)
serving suggestion Make twice the quantity of marinade and serve half as a dipping sauce, if you like.
tips Mirin is a somewhat sweet rice wine used in many Asian, especially Japanese, dishes. You can substitute sherry or sweet white wine for mirin, if you prefer.
Soak bamboo skewers in water for a least 1 hour before use to avoid scorching and splintering during cooking.

slow-roasted turkey with port gravy ENGLAND

4kg turkey
¼ cup (60ml) chicken stock
½ cup (125ml) port
2 tablespoons brown sugar
2 tablespoons olive oil
2 tablespoons plain flour

SEASONING

2 tablespoons olive oil
2 medium brown onions (300g), sliced
500g sausage mince
4 cups (280g) stale breadcrumbs
2 tablespoons chopped fresh sage
½ cup (60g) chopped walnuts

1 Preheat oven to slow. Discard neck and giblets from turkey. Rinse turkey under cold water; pat dry inside and out, tuck wings under body. Spoon seasoning loosely into cavity. Tie legs together with kitchen string.

2 Place turkey into oiled flameproof baking dish; pour stock and half of the port into dish. Cover baking dish tightly with greased foil (if thin, use two layers); bake in slow oven for 5½ hours. Remove foil, brush turkey with combined remaining port and sugar. Increase temperature to moderate; bake, uncovered, 30 minutes or until browned.

3 Remove turkey from dish; cover with foil to keep warm. Strain juices from dish into jug; remove fat from juices. You will need 3 cups (750ml) pan juices. Heat oil in same baking dish, stir in flour; stir over heat until well browned. Remove from heat, gradually stir in reserved pan juices; stir over heat until gravy boils and thickens, strain. Serve turkey with gravy.

seasoning Heat oil in large frying pan, add onion; cook, stirring, until browned, cool. Transfer onion to medium bowl; stir in remaining ingredients.

serves 8

per serving 62.1g fat; 4088kJ (978 cal)

chicken cacciatore ITALY

PREPARATION TIME 30 MINUTES (plus standing time) COOKING TIME 1 HOUR 20 MINUTES

2 tablespoons olive oil

1.5kg chicken pieces

1 medium brown onion (150g),
chopped finely

1 clove garlic, crushed

½ cup (125ml) dry white wine

1½ tablespoons vinegar

½ cup (125ml) chicken stock

400g can tomatoes

1 tablespoon tomato paste

1 teaspoon chopped fresh basil

1 teaspoon sugar

3 anchovy fillets, chopped finely

¼ cup (60ml) milk

60g seeded black olives, halved

1 tablespoon chopped fresh
flat-leaf parsley

1   Preheat oven to moderate. Heat oil in large frying pan; cook chicken until browned all over. Place chicken in ovenproof dish.

2   Pour off most pan juices, leaving about 1 tablespoon in pan. Add onion and garlic to pan; cook until onion is soft. Add wine and vinegar, bring to a boil; boil until reduced by half. Add stock; stir over high heat 2 minutes. Push tomatoes with their liquid through sieve. Add tomatoes to pan with paste, basil and sugar; cook 1 minute.

3   Pour tomato mixture over chicken pieces, cover; cook in moderate oven 1 hour.

4   Soak anchovy in milk 5 minutes; drain on absorbent paper. Arrange chicken pieces on serving dish; keep warm. Pour juices from ovenproof dish into medium saucepan. Bring to a boil; boil 1 minute. Add anchovy, olive and parsley to pan; cook 1 minute. Pour sauce over chicken pieces. Sprinkle with extra chopped parsley, if desired.

serves 4

per serving 40.9g fat; 2470kJ (591 cal)

plum-glazed duck

CHINA

PREPARATION TIME **10 MINUTES** COOKING TIME **1 HOUR 30 MINUTES**

1.8kg duck
3 star anise
2 cloves garlic, peeled
5cm piece fresh ginger, sliced
2 cups (500ml) water

PLUM GLAZE
⅓ cup (80ml) plum sauce
2 tablespoons dark soy sauce
1 teaspoon sesame oil

1 Preheat oven to moderately hot. Fill duck cavity with star anise, garlic and ginger; secure opening with toothpicks. Remove and discard the neck; tie legs loosely together with kitchen string. Place duck, breast-side up, on wire rack in large baking dish; pour the water into baking dish.

2 Roast duck, uncovered, in moderately hot oven 30 minutes. Baste duck all over with plum glaze; cover wing and leg tips with foil. Reduce heat to moderate; roast 30 minutes. Baste again with plum glaze, reduce heat to moderately slow; roast, covered loosely, about 30 minutes or until duck is tender and skin is crisp. Remove toothpicks and string.

3 Cut duck into small pieces to serve.

plum glaze Combine ingredients in small jug.

serves 4

per serving 93.6g fat; 4230kJ (1012 cal)

coq au vin FRANCE

PREPARATION TIME **30 MINUTES** COOKING TIME **55 MINUTES**

This slow-cooked chicken casserole from France is one of the world's best-loved dishes.

800g spring onions
6 bacon rashers (420g)
¼ cup (60ml) olive oil
300g button mushrooms
2 cloves garlic, crushed
8 chicken thigh fillets (880g)
¼ cup (35g) plain flour
2 cups (500ml) dry red wine
1½ cups (375ml) chicken stock
2 tablespoons tomato paste
3 bay leaves
4 sprigs fresh thyme
2 sprigs fresh rosemary

1 Trim green ends from onions, leaving about 4cm of stem attached; trim roots. Remove rind from bacon, cut bacon into 3cm pieces. Heat 1 tablespoon of the oil in large frying pan; cook onion, stirring, until browned all over, remove from pan. Add bacon, mushrooms and garlic to same pan; cook, stirring, until bacon is crisp, remove from pan.

2 Toss chicken in flour; shake off excess. Heat remaining oil in same pan. Cook chicken, in batches, until browned all over; drain on absorbent paper.

3 Return chicken to pan with wine, stock, paste, bay leaves, herbs, onion, and bacon and mushroom mixture. Bring to a boil; simmer, uncovered, about 35 minutes or until chicken is tender and sauce has thickened slightly. Remove bay leaves before serving.

serves 4

per serving 34.8g fat; 3072kJ (735 cal)
serving suggestion Serve with crusty french bread.

roast chicken   ENGLAND

PREPARATION TIME **30 MINUTES**   COOKING TIME **1 HOUR 45 MINUTES** (plus standing time)

Use kitchen string for trussing the chicken; it is strong and will not melt in a hot oven.

1.5kg chicken
15g butter, melted

SEASONING
1½ cups (105g) stale breadcrumbs
1 trimmed stick celery (75g),
    chopped finely
1 small white onion (80g),
    chopped finely
1 teaspoon dried mixed herbs
1 egg, beaten lightly
30g butter, melted

1 Preheat oven to moderately hot. Remove and discard any fat from cavity of chicken.

2 Fill cavity of chicken with seasoning; do not pack in tightly because bread expands during cooking and the seasoning will become a solid mass.

3 Place chicken on board, breast-side up. Secure chicken with kitchen string by looping string around tail end; bring string around ends of drumsticks. Following the creases between drumsticks and body, take string towards wing end of chicken.

4 Turn chicken breast-side down and secure string around wings.

5 Place chicken on rack over baking dish. Half-fill baking dish with water; it should not touch the chicken. Using small pastry brush, brush chicken with butter; bake in moderately hot oven 15 minutes. Reduce heat to moderate; bake 1½ hours. Pierce skin and flesh of chicken in thickest part of drumstick; the juices will be clear if chicken is cooked. Stand chicken 10 minutes before breaking or cutting into serving-sized pieces.

seasoning Combine ingredients in medium bowl; mix well.

serves 4

per serving 35.4g fat; 2349kJ (562 cal)

chicken tagine with dates and honey

MIDDLE-EAST

PREPARATION TIME 25 MINUTES   COOKING TIME 1 HOUR 45 MINUTES

1kg chicken thigh fillets
2 tablespoons olive oil
2 medium brown onions (300g),
   sliced thinly
4 cloves garlic, crushed
1 teaspoon cumin seeds
1 teaspoon ground coriander
1 teaspoon ground ginger
1 teaspoon ground turmeric
1 teaspoon ground cinnamon
½ teaspoon chilli powder
¼ teaspoon ground nutmeg
1½ cups (375ml) chicken stock
1 cup (250ml) water
½ cup (85g) seedless dates, halved
¼ cup (90g) honey
½ cup (80g) blanched almonds, toasted
1 tablespoon chopped fresh coriander

1 Cut chicken into 3cm strips. Heat 1 tablespoon of the oil in medium saucepan; cook chicken, in batches, stirring, until browned. Drain chicken on absorbent paper.

2 Heat remaining oil in same pan, add onion, garlic and spices; cook, stirring, until onion is soft.

3 Return chicken to pan with stock and the water; simmer, covered, 1 hour. Remove lid, simmer about 30 minutes or until mixture is thickened slightly and chicken is tender. Stir in dates, honey and nuts; sprinkle with coriander.

serves 4

per serving 40.2g fat; 2855kJ (683 cal)
tip Chicken tagine can be made three hours ahead and stored, covered, in the refrigerator; the tagine is also suitable to freeze, without the nuts and coriander.

green chicken curry THAILAND

PREPARATION TIME 25 MINUTES   COOKING TIME 15 MINUTES

750g chicken thigh fillets
200g green beans
1 cup (250ml) coconut cream

GREEN CURRY PASTE
3 small fresh green chillies, chopped
3 green onions, chopped
2 cloves garlic, crushed
¼ cup chopped fresh lemon grass
¼ cup chopped fresh coriander
2 tablespoons peanut oil
2 tablespoons water
1 teaspoon shrimp paste
½ teaspoon ground cumin
¼ teaspoon ground turmeric

1 Cut chicken into thin strips. Chop beans. Cook green curry paste in heated medium saucepan, stirring, about 3 minutes or until fragrant.

2 Add chicken and beans to pan; cook, stirring, about 5 minutes or until chicken is tender. Stir in coconut cream; simmer, uncovered, about 3 minutes or until slightly thickened.

green curry paste Blend or process ingredients until smooth.

serves 4

per serving 35.8g fat; 2027kJ (485 cal)
tip The green curry paste can be made a week ahead; store, covered, in the refrigerator.

mainsvegetarian

mixed dhal

INDIA

PREPARATION TIME **15 MINUTES** COOKING TIME **1 HOUR 15 MINUTES**

60g ghee
2 medium brown onions (300g), chopped finely
2 cloves garlic, crushed
1 tablespoon grated fresh ginger
2 tablespoons black mustard seeds
2 tablespoons ground cumin
1 tablespoon ground coriander
2 teaspoons ground turmeric
¾ cup (150g) brown lentils
¾ cup (150g) red lentils
¾ cup (150g) yellow split peas
¾ cup (150g) green split peas
2 x 400g cans tomatoes
1 litre (4 cups) vegetable stock
⅔ cup (160ml) coconut cream
½ cup coarsely chopped fresh coriander

1 Heat ghee in large heavy-based saucepan; cook onion, garlic
   and ginger, stirring, until onion is soft. Add seeds and spices;
   cook, stirring, until fragrant.

2 Add lentils and peas to pan; stir to combine. Add undrained
   crushed tomatoes and stock; bring to a boil. Simmer, covered,
   about 1 hour, stirring occasionally, until lentils are tender
   and mixture thickens.

3 Just before serving, add coconut cream and coriander; stir over
   low heat until dhal is heated through.

serves 8

per serving 13.9g fat; 1480kJ (353 cal)
serving suggestion Serve with steamed basmati rice and homemade roti.
tip Clarify ordinary butter if ghee is unavailable by heating butter in
small pan until white sediment comes to the surface; skim and discard
sediment, using the remaining heavy "oil".

fettuccine alfredo   ITALY

PREPARATION TIME 5 MINUTES COOKING TIME 15 MINUTES

375g fettuccine
90g butter
⅔ cup (160ml) cream
1 cup (80g) grated parmesan cheese
1 tablespoon chopped fresh
**   flat-leaf parsley**

1 Cook pasta in large saucepan of boiling water until tender; drain.

2 Meanwhile, heat butter and cream in medium frying pan until butter melts; remove from heat. Add cheese and parsley; stir until sauce is blended and smooth.

3 Combine sauce and pasta; sprinkle with extra chopped parsley, if desired.

serves 4

per serving 39.8g fat; 2939kJ (703 cal)
tip This recipe is best made just before serving.

spaghetti with pesto   ITALY

PREPARATION TIME **15 MINUTES** COOKING TIME **10 MINUTES**

⅓ cup (80ml) olive oil
2 tablespoons pine nuts
2 cups (75g) coarsely chopped
**   fresh basil**
2 cloves garlic
¼ cup (20g) grated parmesan cheese
375g spaghetti

1   Place 1 tablespoon of the oil in medium frying pan. Cook pine nuts, over low heat, until browned lightly; drain immediately on absorbent paper.

2   Blend or process basil, pine nuts and garlic until well combined. With motor operating, add remaining oil in thin stream; process until combined.

3   Place basil mixture in medium bowl. Add cheese; mix well.

4   Meanwhile, cook pasta in large saucepan of boiling water until tender; drain. Combine pesto and pasta.

serves 4

per serving   26.1g fat; 2337kJ (588 cal)

tip   The basil mixture can be frozen without the addition of the cheese; add cheese just before serving.

ratatouille FRANCE

PREPARATION TIME **20 MINUTES (plus standing time)**   COOKING TIME **30 MINUTES**

A popular dish from Provence, France, ratatouille (pronounced ra-tuh-too-ee) makes a brilliant vegetarian meal when served with bread or couscous; it can also be served as an accompaniment to grilled meat, fish or chicken.

1 medium eggplant (300g), chopped
1 teaspoon salt
1 medium red onion (170g)
2 tablespoons olive oil
1 clove garlic, crushed
1 small red capsicum (150g),
**   chopped coarsely**
1 small green capsicum (150g),
**   chopped coarsely**
2 medium zucchinis (240g),
**   sliced thickly**
400g can tomatoes
1 tablespoon tomato paste
1 tablespoon chopped fresh oregano

1   Place eggplant in a colander, sprinkle with salt and stand for 15 minutes. Rinse eggplant under cold water, drain well; pat dry with absorbent paper.

2   Cut onion into thin wedges. Heat half of the oil in large frying pan, add onion, garlic and capsicums; cook, stirring, about 5 minutes or until onion is soft. Remove onion mixture from pan.

3   Heat remaining oil in same pan, add eggplant and zucchini; cook, stirring, about 5 minutes or until eggplant is browned lightly.

4   Return onion mixture to pan, add undrained crushed tomatoes and paste; simmer, covered, about 20 minutes or until vegetables are tender. Stir in oregano.

serves 4

per serving   10.2g fat; 614kJ (147 cal)

spaghetti napoletana ITALY

2 x 400g cans tomatoes
30g butter
1 tablespoon olive oil
2 cloves garlic, crushed
1 tablespoon shredded fresh basil
2 tablespoons chopped fresh
    flat-leaf parsley
250g spaghetti

1 Push tomatoes, with their liquid, through sieve.

2 Heat butter and oil in large saucepan, add garlic; cook, stirring, 1 minute. Add pureed tomato; bring to a boil. Reduce heat; simmer, uncovered, about 40 minutes or until sauce reduces by about half. Stir in basil and parsley.

3 Meanwhile, cook pasta in large saucepan of boiling water until tender; drain. Combine sauce and pasta.

serves 2

per serving 23.6g fat; 2750kJ (658 cal)

gnocchi alla romana   ITALY

PREPARATION TIME 30 MINUTES (plus refrigeration time)   COOKING TIME 40 MINUTES

3 cups (750ml) milk
1 teaspoon salt
pinch ground nutmeg
⅔ cup (110g) semolina
1 egg, beaten lightly
1½ cups (120g) grated
  parmesan cheese
60g butter, melted

1 Bring milk, salt and nutmeg to a boil in medium saucepan; reduce heat. Gradually add semolina, stirring constantly with wooden spoon. Cook semolina mixture, uncovered, stirring often, about 10 minutes or until spoon can stand unsupported in the semolina. Remove from heat.

2 Combine egg and 1 cup of the cheese in small bowl. Add to semolina mixture; stir well. Spread mixture onto well-oiled 26cm x 32cm swiss roll pan; using wet spatula, smooth until 5mm thick. Refrigerate about 1 hour or until semolina is firm.

3 Cut semolina into circles using 4cm cutter. Arrange circles, overlapping, in greased shallow ovenproof dish. Pour over butter; sprinkle with remaining cheese. Bake in moderate oven about 15 minutes or until crisp and golden.

serves 4

per serving 31.1g fat; 1990kJ (476 cal)

asparagus risotto   ITALY

PREPARATION TIME **15 MINUTES**   COOKING TIME **45 MINUTES**

500g fresh asparagus
30g butter
1 tablespoon olive oil
1 large brown onion (200g), chopped
1 clove garlic, crushed
1¾ cups (350g) arborio rice
3 cups (750ml) vegetable stock
3 cups (750ml) water
¾ cup (60g) grated parmesan cheese
2 tablespoons chopped fresh
**   flat-leaf parsley**

1 Cut asparagus into 2.5cm lengths. Boil, steam or microwave asparagus until just tender; drain, rinse under cold water, drain well. Heat butter and oil in pan, add onion and garlic; cook, stirring, until onion is soft. Add rice, stir until combined.

2 Meanwhile, combine stock and the water in another pan, bring to a boil; keep hot. Stir ⅔ cup (160ml) hot stock mixture into rice mixture; cook, stirring, over low heat until liquid is absorbed. Continue adding stock mixture very gradually, stirring until absorbed before each addition. Total cooking time should be about 30 minutes or until rice is tender. Stir in asparagus, cheese and parsley, stir until hot.

serves 4

per serving   17g fat; 2187kJ (522 cal)

eggplant parmigiana   ITALY

PREPARATION TIME **35 MINUTES**   COOKING TIME **2 HOURS 20 MINUTES**

This delicious eggplant dish is best served with a short, fat, hollow pasta, such as shells.

**1 medium brown onion (150g),
    chopped finely**
**2 trimmed celery sticks (150g),
    chopped finely**
2 tablespoons brandy
**2 tablespoons chopped fresh
    flat-leaf parsley**
3 cups (750g) tomato pasta sauce
2 litres (8 cups) water
1 teaspoon sugar
vegetable oil, for shallow-frying
2 large eggplants (1kg), sliced thickly
¾ cup (75g) packaged breadcrumbs
½ cup (40g) grated romano cheese
1kg shell pasta

1   Heat large heavy-based saucepan; cook onion and celery, stirring, until onion is soft. Add brandy and parsley; cook, stirring, until most of the brandy evaporates. Stir in sauce, the water and sugar; simmer, uncovered, about 1¼ hours or until mixture thickens slightly.

2   Meanwhile, heat oil in large frying pan; shallow-fry eggplant, in batches, until browned both sides. Drain on absorbent paper.

3   Preheat oven to moderate. Place one-third of the eggplant, in a single layer, in shallow 3-litre (12 cup) ovenproof dish; pour one-third of the tomato mixture over eggplant, sprinkle with half of the breadcrumbs and half of the cheese. Repeat layering process, finishing with eggplant and tomato mixture.

4   Bake eggplant parmigiana, uncovered, in moderate oven about 40 minutes or until almost set.

5   Just before serving, cook pasta in large saucepan of boiling water, uncovered, until just tender; drain. Serve eggplant parmigiana over pasta.

serves 8

per serving 12.5g fat; 2709kJ (648 cal)
serving suggestion Serve with veal schnitzel.
tip Eggplant can be sprayed lightly with cooking-oil spray and browned under a grill for a lower-fat version.

potato and onion bhaji INDIA

PREPARATION TIME **15 MINUTES** COOKING TIME **15 MINUTES**

45g ghee
1 teaspoon brown mustard seeds
2 medium leeks (700g), sliced thinly
2 large brown onions (400g),
   sliced thinly
2 medium potatoes (400g),
   sliced thinly
1 medium carrot (120g), sliced thinly
1 teaspoon grated fresh ginger
½ teaspoon cumin seeds
½ teaspoon ground turmeric
¼ teaspoon chilli powder
1 teaspoon garam masala
1 teaspoon salt

1 Heat ghee in large heavy-based frying pan, add mustard seeds; cook, stirring, 30 seconds.

2 Stir in leek, onion, potato, carrot, ginger, cumin seeds, turmeric and chilli powder; cook, stirring, 5 minutes.

3 Add garam masala and salt, cover; cook over low heat 10 minutes or until vegetables are tender.

serves 6

per serving 8.3g fat; 606kJ (145 cal)

vegetable tempura   JAPAN

PREPARATION TIME **20 MINUTES**   COOKING TIME **20 MINUTES**

Always use fresh, clean oil for this dish and keep at a constant temperature during cooking. The optimum temperature for cooking vegetables is fairly hot, about 170°C.

1 medium brown onion (150g)
1 small fresh or frozen lotus root (200g)
8 fresh shiitake mushrooms
2 sheets toasted seaweed (yaki-nori)
20g cellophane noodles, cut in half
vegetable oil, for deep-frying
120g pumpkin, sliced thinly
50g green beans, halved
1 small kumara (250g), sliced thinly
1 baby eggplant (60g), sliced thinly
1 small red capsicum (150g),
**   seeded, cut into squares**
1 medium carrot (120g),
**   sliced thinly, diagonally**
250g firm tofu, cut into 2cm cubes
plain flour
1 lemon, cut into wedges

BATTER
1 egg, beaten lightly
2 cups (500ml) iced soda water
1 cup (150g) plain flour
1 cup (150g) cornflour

DIPPING SAUCE
1 cup (250ml) dashi
⅓ cup (80ml) mirin
⅓ cup (80ml) light soy sauce
½ cup (120g) finely grated daikon,
**   drained well**
3 teaspoons grated fresh ginger

1 Halve onion from root end. Insert toothpicks at regular intervals to hold onion rings together and slice in between.

2 Peel lotus root and slice. Place in water with a dash of vinegar to prevent browning. If using canned lotus, drain and slice. Remove and discard mushroom stems; cut a cross in the top of caps.

3 Cut one sheet seaweed into 5cm squares, halve the other sheet and cut into 2cm-wide strips. Brush seaweed strips with water and wrap tightly around about 10 noodles, either at one end or in the middle; reserve noodle bunches.

4 Heat oil to moderately hot. Dust ingredients, except seaweed squares and lemon, lightly in flour; shake off excess flour. Dip one side of seaweed squares, and other ingredients wholly, in batter, drain excess batter; deep-fry ingredients, in batches, until golden. Drain on absorbent paper. Only fry small amounts at a time and make sure enough time is allowed for oil to come back to correct temperature before adding next batch.

5 Finally, deep-fry reserved noodle bundles and serve as a garnish.

6 Serve immediately with lemon wedges and individual bowls of warm dipping sauce.

batter Combine egg in a bowl with iced water. Add sifted flours all at once, mixing lightly until just combined, but still very lumpy.

dipping sauce Combine dashi, mirin and sauce in medium saucepan and heat gently. Divide among four individual serving bowls. Shape daikon into four pyramid shapes. Place a pyramid in each serving bowl; top with even amounts of ginger.

serves 4

per serving 39.1g fat; 3269kJ (782 cal)
tips Always use iced or chilled water in the batter; make the batter just before beginning to deep-fry. Never mix batter well; it should have lumps of dry flour through it with a ring of flour around the edges of the bowl. Use absorbent paper to dry all of the foods to be coated. Seaweed is never floured and only battered on one side or flavour and texture is lost. To test if oil is the correct temperature, drop a small amount of batter into oil. If it drops just below the surface then bounces back, the oil is ready.

salads

These classic salads are nothing if not versatile – offerings from Mexico and Thailand make perfectly filling main meals, others (from Greece and the Middle-East) are delicious accompaniments to a main course, and yet others, with their origins in Italy and Latin America, make tasty starters.

fattoush MIDDLE-EAST

PREPARATION TIME **15 MINUTES** COOKING TIME **15 MINUTES (plus cooling time)**

Most cultures have a salad that incorporates yesterday's bread as an ingredient (rather than wasting it), and fattoush is a delectable Middle-Eastern version. Purslane, a leafy green that grows wild, is also commonly called pigweed and can be hard to find in shops; substitute it with baby rocket leaves in this recipe.

2 large pieces pitta

1 tablespoon olive oil

**2 lebanese cucumbers (260g),
    sliced thinly**

**4 medium tomatoes (760g),
    sliced thinly**

3 green onions, sliced thinly

**1 medium green capsicum (200g),
    chopped finely**

1 cup chopped fresh flat-leaf parsley

¼ cup chopped fresh mint

1 cup chopped fresh purslane

2 tablespoons olive oil, extra

¼ cup (60ml) lemon juice

1 clove garlic, crushed

1 Preheat oven to moderately hot. Brush both sides of bread with the oil, place on oven tray; toast in moderately hot oven about 15 minutes or until crisp. Cool; break bread into small pieces.

2 Combine cucumber, tomato, onion, capsicum and herbs in large bowl. Just before serving, add bread; drizzle fattoush with combined extra oil, juice and garlic.

serves 4

per serving 15.9g fat; 1325kJ (317 cal)

serving suggestion Fattoush is usually served, rather than the more common tabbouleh, as part of a mezze; it's also good served with "ful medames" – dried broad beans stewed with lashings of garlic and lemon juice until almost a puree.

tip The toasted pitta pieces can be made a day ahead; store in an airtight container until needed.

ceviche LATIN AMERICA

PREPARATION TIME **15 MINUTES (plus refrigeration time)**

Ceviche, also known as seviche or cebiche, is an everyday fish salad eaten all over Latin America. You will need approximately 10 limes for this recipe. The lime juice "cooks" the fish.

1kg redfish fillets
1½ cups (375ml) fresh lime juice
¼ cup (40g) canned jalapeño chilli slices, drained
¼ cup (60ml) olive oil
1 large tomato (250g), chopped coarsely
¼ cup chopped fresh coriander
1 small white onion (80g), chopped finely
1 clove garlic, crushed

1 Remove any remaining skin or bones from fish; cut fish into 3cm pieces.

2 Combine fish and juice in non-reactive large bowl, cover; refrigerate overnight.

3 Drain fish; discard juice. Return fish to bowl, add remaining ingredients; toss gently to combine. Cover; refrigerate 1 hour.

serves 4

per serving 19.1g fat; 1689kJ (404 cal)
tip Fish must be marinated with the lime juice in a non-reactive bowl (one made from glazed porcelain or glass is best), to avoid the metallic taste that can result if marinating takes place in a stainless-steel or an aluminium bowl. Ensure all of the fish is completely covered with juice.

rocket and parmesan salad ITALY

PREPARATION TIME **25 MINUTES** COOKING TIME **3 MINUTES**

This salad is found on the menus of Italian restaurants everywhere in the world. The combination of the rocket's appealing bitterness and the sweet acidity of the balsamic vinegar offer a welcome foil to the richness of many Italian main courses.

60g parmesan cheese
200g baby rocket leaves
80g semi-dried tomatoes,
   halved lengthways
¼ cup (40g) pine nuts, toasted
¼ cup (60ml) balsamic vinegar
¼ cup (60ml) extra virgin olive oil

1 Using vegetable peeler, shave cheese into wide, long pieces.

2 Combine rocket with tomato and nuts in large bowl; add cheese, drizzle with combined vinegar and oil, toss gently.

serves 8

per serving 14g fat; 686kJ (164 cal)

tips Baby spinach leaves can be substituted for rocket. Nuts of any kind can easily be toasted on top of the stove by stirring them in a dry heavy-based pan over medium-to-high heat briefly, until they are just golden brown.

hot potato salad   GERMANY

PREPARATION TIME **10 MINUTES**   COOKING TIME **15 MINUTES (plus cooling time)**

Typical hearty German fare, this classic salad has been made easier to prepare by the addition of ready-made mayonnaise.

4 eggs
4 bacon rashers (280g), chopped
750g tiny new potatoes
2 pickled gherkins, chopped finely
1 tablespoon chopped fresh
   flat-leaf parsley
⅔ cup (200g) mayonnaise
⅓ cup (80g) sour cream
2 teaspoons lemon juice

1 Cover eggs with water in medium saucepan; bring to a boil. Simmer, uncovered, 10 minutes; drain. Cool eggs under cold water; shell and chop coarsely.

2 Meanwhile, fry bacon, uncovered, in dry heated frying pan until browned and crisp; drain on absorbent paper.

3 Boil, steam or microwave potatoes until tender; drain and halve.

4 Combine remaining ingredients in large pan; stir over low heat until just hot. Place mayonnaise mixture in large bowl with potato, bacon and egg; toss gently to combine.

serves 4

per serving 32.3g fat; 2215kJ (530 cal)
serving suggestion This warm, satisfying salad is great served with grilled pork chops and hot and sour red cabbage.
tip Bacon can be fried and eggs hard-boiled a few hours beforehand.

chicken and cabbage salad VIETNAM

This dish, known as ga xe phai, is one of Vietnam's most popular salads. You need to purchase one small chinese cabbage as well as a large barbecued chicken, weighing approximately 900g, for this recipe.

100g snow peas, trimmed
4 cups (400g) shredded chicken
4 cups (320g) finely shredded
**   chinese cabbage**
4 garlic chives, chopped finely
1 medium red onion (170g),
**   sliced thinly**
½ cup chopped fresh mint
1 teaspoon sambal oelek
1 tablespoon sesame oil
⅓ cup (80ml) lime juice
⅓ cup (80ml) fish sauce
2 teaspoons sugar
½ cup loosely packed fresh coriander

1 Place snow peas in medium bowl. Cover with boiling water; drain immediately. Cover snow peas with cold water in same bowl; stand 2 minutes. Drain; slice thinly.

2 Combine snow peas in large bowl with chicken, cabbage, chives, onion and mint.

3 Combine sambal, oil, juice, sauce and sugar in screw-top jar; shake well. Drizzle salad with dressing; toss gently to combine then sprinkle coriander over salad.

serves 4

per serving 13.6g fat; 1158kJ (277 cal)
serving suggestion Serve with puffed prawn crackers.

chicken larb THAILAND

PREPARATION TIME **20 MINUTES** COOKING TIME **15 MINUTES**

This delicious Thai salad originates from the north-western province around Chiang Mai; it can be made with beef or pork mince as well as the chicken version given below.

2 tablespoons peanut oil
1 tablespoon finely chopped
    fresh lemon grass
2 fresh red thai chillies, seeded,
    chopped finely
1 clove garlic, crushed
1 tablespoon grated fresh ginger
750g chicken mince
4 kaffir lime leaves
1 tablespoon fish sauce
⅓ cup (80ml) lime juice
1 medium white onion (150g),
    sliced thinly
1 cup loosely packed fresh
    coriander leaves
1¼ cups (100g) bean sprouts,
    tips trimmed
½ cup loosely packed fresh
    thai basil leaves
½ cup loosely packed fresh
    vietnamese mint leaves
100g watercress
1 medium green cucumber (170g),
    sliced thinly

1 Heat half of the oil in large frying pan; cook lemon grass, chilli, garlic and ginger, stirring, until fragrant. Add chicken; cook, stirring, about 10 minutes or until cooked through.

2 Add torn kaffir lime leaves, half of the fish sauce and half of the lime juice; cook, stirring, 5 minutes.

3 Combine onion, coriander, sprouts, basil, mint, watercress and cucumber in large bowl; drizzle with combined remaining fish sauce, juice and oil, toss salad mixture gently.

4 Place salad mixture on serving plate; top with chicken mixture.

serves 4

per serving 25.1g fat; 1676kJ (401 cal)
serving suggestion Hot and sour soup is a good opening act for a big platter of larb.
tip Add the chicken mince to the frying pan in batches, stirring between additions, so chicken doesn't clump.

spicy beef salad   THAILAND

PREPARATION TIME 25 MINUTES   COOKING TIME 7 MINUTES (plus standing time)

400g beef rump steak

2 small white onions (160g), sliced thinly

2 lebanese cucumbers (260g), seeded, sliced thinly

1 fresh red thai chilli, seeded, sliced thinly

250g cherry tomatoes, halved

¼ cup loosely packed fresh basil leaves

¼ cup loosely packed fresh coriander leaves

¼ cup loosely packed fresh vietnamese mint leaves

GARLIC DRESSING

2 fresh red thai chillies, seeded, chopped coarsely

2 tablespoons coarsely chopped fresh lemon grass

⅔ cup firmly packed fresh coriander

3 cloves garlic, chopped coarsely

⅓ cup (80ml) lime juice

1 tablespoon fish sauce

1 tablespoon soy sauce

1   Cook beef in heated oiled grill pan (or on grill or barbecue) until browned both sides and cooked as desired; cover, stand 10 minutes, slice thinly.

2   Just before serving, gently toss beef, remaining ingredients and dressing in large bowl.

garlic dressing   Blend or process ingredients until smooth.

serves 4

per serving 7g fat; 961kJ (230 cal)

serving suggestion   This is a great first course when you feel like preparing a special Thai banquet for your friends.

tip   If you're a chilli fan, you can increase the heat of this dish by adding more than one chilli.

tomato, olive and fetta salad GREECE

PREPARATION TIME 25 MINUTES

Dried rigani, which resembles dried oregano but has longer leaves and is grey-green in colour, can be purchased in Greek and Middle-Eastern food shops. If you can't find it in your area, substitute a mixture of fresh or dried oregano and/or marjoram, but adjust the amount used to suit your taste.

4 medium egg tomatoes (300g)
2 lebanese cucumbers (260g)
1 medium red onion (170g)
2 medium green capsicums (400g),
    sliced thinly
1 cup (160g) kalamata olives
150g sheep-milk fetta cheese
1 teaspoon crushed dried rigani
½ cup (125ml) extra virgin olive oil

1 Quarter tomatoes and cucumbers lengthways; cut into chunks. Cut onion into wedges.

2 Combine tomato, cucumber, onion, capsicum and olives in large serving bowl.

3 Break cheese into large pieces and toss through salad, sprinkle with rigani; drizzle with oil.

serves 4

per serving 39.6g fat; 2738kJ (655 cal)
serving suggestion This salad is ideal with barbecued seafood; in Greece, barbecued octopus is usually served with it. It's also good with grilled lamb skewers.
tips For an authentic Greek way of presenting this salad, leave the fetta in a whole piece and sit it on the top of the salad.

tabbouleh   MIDDLE-EAST

PREPARATION TIME **40 MINUTES (plus refrigeration time)**

Tabbouleh is one Middle-Eastern salad we're all familiar with these days – besides being absolutely delicious, it's one of the most nutritionally sound dishes we can think of, containing plenty of fibre as well as a healthy dose of vitamin C.

3 medium tomatoes (570g)
½ cup (80g) burghul
5 cups firmly packed fresh
 flat-leaf parsley
1 medium red onion (170g)
1 cup firmly packed fresh mint leaves
¼ cup (60ml) lemon juice
¼ cup (60ml) extra virgin olive oil

1 Chop tomatoes finely, retaining as much of the juice as possible. Place tomato and juice on top of burghul in small bowl, cover; refrigerate at least 2 hours or until burghul is soft.

2 Meanwhile, cut parsley coarsely with scissors or chop coarsely with knife; chop onion finely and chop mint coarsely.

3 Combine parsley, onion and mint in large bowl with burghul-tomato mixture and remaining ingredients; toss gently to combine.

serves 4

per serving 15.3g fat; 1028kJ (246 cal)

serving suggestion Tabbouleh is the ideal accompaniment to any Middle-Eastern meal. Serve it with garlic chicken, beef or lamb skewers, or baked fish.

tip Burghul, often mistakenly thought to be the same as cracked wheat, is a wheat kernel that has been steamed, dried and crushed. It comes in a variety of grinds – coarse, medium and fine – and can be bought from health food stores, delicatessens and supermarkets under various names: bulgar, bulghur wheat or lebanese crushed wheat. Do not substitute with ordinary unprocessed cracked wheat.

tomato and bocconcini salad   ITALY

PREPARATION TIME **10 MINUTES**

4 medium tomatoes (520g)
350g large bocconcini cheese
¼ cup shredded fresh basil

DRESSING
¼ cup (60ml) extra virgin olive oil
2 teaspoons balsamic vinegar
1 clove garlic, crushed
1 teaspoon caster sugar

1 Cut tomatoes into 5mm slices. Break bocconcini into large chunks.

2 Layer tomatoes and bocconcini alternately on serving plate; sprinkle with basil and dressing.

dressing Combine ingredients in screw-top jar; shake well.

serves 4

per serving 27.7g fat; 1372kJ (328 cal)

tip This recipe can be made three hours ahead; store, covered, in the refrigerator.

gado gado

INDONESIA

PREPARATION TIME **20 MINUTES**   COOKING TIME **15 MINUTES**

Gado gado translates roughly as "mixed mixed", which explains the casual way that Indonesians eat this salad. Drizzle vegetables with the sauce and let everyone help themselves. Gado gado can either be served at room temperature or cold.

4 cups (320g) finely shredded chinese cabbage
8 baby new potatoes (320g)
2 trimmed corn cobs (500g), sliced thickly
200g green beans, halved
1 large carrot (180g), sliced thinly
2 lebanese cucumbers (260g), sliced diagonally
1 small pineapple (800g), chopped coarsely
2 cups (160g) bean sprouts
150g fried tofu, chopped coarsely
4 hard-boiled eggs, halved

PEANUT SAUCE
1⅓ cups (375g) crunchy peanut butter
1 cup (250ml) chicken stock
2 tablespoons light soy sauce
1 tablespoon lemon juice
1 teaspoon sambal oelek
1 clove garlic, crushed
2 teaspoons sugar
½ cup (125ml) coconut milk

1   Boil, steam or microwave cabbage, potatoes, corn, beans and carrot, separately, until vegetables are just tender. Chop potatoes coarsely.

2   Arrange cooked vegetables, cucumber, pineapple, sprouts, tofu and egg on serving platter. Serve gado gado with peanut sauce.

peanut sauce   Combine peanut butter, stock, sauce, juice, sambal, garlic and sugar in medium saucepan; bring to a boil. Reduce heat; simmer, stirring, about 1 minute or until sauce thickens slightly. Add coconut milk; stir until hot. Pour sauce into serving bowl.

serves 4

per serving   63.4g fat; 4063kJ (972 cal)
serving suggestion   Serve as a light lunch with freshly puffed prawn crackers, or as a more substantial meal with boiled rice and a meat dish.
tip   We used packaged fried tofu, available from supermarkets; however, you can shallow-fry cubes of firm tofu in vegetable oil until browned lightly, then drain on absorbent paper, if preferred.

panzanella   ITALY

PREPARATION TIME 25 MINUTES

Panzanella is a traditional Italian bread salad that probably came about as a way of using up yesterday's bread. For this recipe, we used ciabatta, a wood-fired white loaf readily available from most supermarkets. Any Italian crusty bread may be used in its place.

1 loaf stale ciabatta
6 medium tomatoes (1.1kg)
2 trimmed sticks celery (150g)
1 lebanese cucumber (130g)
1 medium red onion (170g),
  chopped coarsely
½ cup firmly packed fresh basil leaves
¼ cup (60ml) red wine vinegar
½ cup (125ml) olive oil
1 clove garlic, crushed

1 Cut ciabatta in half horizontally; reserve one half for another use. Remove and discard soft centre from remaining half; cut remaining bread into 2cm pieces.

2 Cut tomatoes into wedges. Discard seeds; chop coarsely.

3 Cut celery into four strips lengthways; chop strips coarsely.

4 Cut cucumber in half lengthways; cut halves into 2cm-thick slices.

5 Combine onion with bread, tomato, celery, cucumber and basil in large bowl.

6 Combine remaining ingredients in screw-top jar; shake well. Pour dressing over salad; toss gently.

serves 4

per serving 33.3g fat; 2562kJ (613 cal)

salade niçoise FRANCE

PREPARATION TIME **10 MINUTES**

The original "salade niçoise" from the French Mediterranean city of Nice, was made of the best of that region's produce; ripe vine tomatoes, local capers, hand-picked baby beans, tiny dark brown olives, anchovies and tuna fresh from the sea, and plump cloves of garlic. No wonder it so delighted foreign visitors to Nice that they took the memory of that salad to all corners of the globe, adapting it slightly, as we have here, to suit their own produce and lifestyle.

3 x 125g cans tuna slices in springwater, drained
1 medium red onion (170g), sliced thinly
250g baby spinach leaves, trimmed
300g can white beans, rinsed, drained
150g yellow teardrop tomatoes, halved
½ cup (80g) kalamata olives, seeded
4 hard-boiled eggs, quartered

DRESSING
½ cup (125ml) extra virgin olive oil
¼ cup (60ml) lemon juice
1 clove garlic, crushed
1 teaspoon chopped fresh lemon thyme
2 teaspoons dijon mustard
¼ teaspoon sugar

1 Combine ingredients in large bowl.

2 Just before serving, pour dressing over salad mixture; toss gently to combine.

dressing Combine ingredients in screw-top jar; shake well.

serves 4

per serving 38.1g fat; 2065kJ (494 cal)

tips If you gently stir the eggs until they begin to boil, you will have nicely centred yolks – a good look when they're to be served quartered, as they are here.
If you want to make this dish really special, substitute the canned tuna with about 450g of fresh tuna steaks, brushed with lemon and oil, then pan-fried or grilled and cut into bite-sized pieces.

caesar salad   MEXICO

PREPARATION TIME **25 MINUTES**   COOKING TIME **5 MINUTES**

This universally loved salad is thought to have originated in Tijuana, Mexico, in the 1920s, in a restaurant owned by an Italian chef by the name of Caesar Cardini.

7 slices thick white bread
2 tablespoons light olive oil
100g parmesan cheese
1 large cos lettuce
5 whole canned anchovy fillets,
    drained, halved lengthways

CAESAR DRESSING
1 egg
1 clove garlic, crushed
2 tablespoons lemon juice
½ teaspoon dijon mustard
5 whole canned anchovy fillets, drained
¾ cup (180ml) light olive oil

1 Discard crusts; cut bread into 1cm cubes. Heat oil in large frying pan; cook bread, stirring, until browned and crisp. Drain croutons on absorbent paper.

2 Using vegetable peeler, shave cheese into long thin pieces.

3 Combine torn lettuce leaves with half of the croutons, half of the anchovies and half of the cheese in large bowl; add half of the dressing, mix well. Sprinkle remaining croutons, anchovies and cheese over salad; drizzle with remaining dressing.

caesar dressing   Blend or process egg, garlic, juice, mustard and anchovies until smooth; with motor operating, add oil in thin stream, process until dressing thickens.

serves 4

per serving   62.1g fat; 3076kJ (736 cal)
serving suggestion   Caesar salad can be served as a light meal on its own or, as you see in many restaurants, with pieces of grilled chicken breast tossed in with the dressing.

tip   The caesar dressing can be made a day ahead; store, covered, in the refrigerator.

coleslaw USA

PREPARATION TIME **10 MINUTES**

This recipe for coleslaw is a basic one to which you can add many other ingredients to suit your taste. You can use any type of cabbage; the traditional one is the firm, white drumhead cabbage; the curly savoy or even chinese cabbage will also give good results. Slice the cabbage as finely as you like.

½ **small cabbage (600g)**
1 **medium carrot (120g), grated coarsely**
4 **green onions, sliced thinly**
¼ **cup (75g) mayonnaise**
2 **teaspoons lemon juice**

1 Using sharp knife, remove core from cabbage; shred cabbage finely.

2 Combine cabbage, carrot and onion in large bowl, add combined mayonnaise and juice, mix well.

serves 4

per serving 6.3g fat; 443kJ (106 cal)

accompaniments

Many of these accompaniments are great stand-alone snacks;
some, particularly hash browns and rösti, make ideal breakfasts.
The majority, though, are the perfect complement to a main meal,
and have origins in countries as far flung as India and Switzerland.

stir-fried asian greens CHINA

PREPARATION TIME **10 MINUTES** COOKING TIME **10 MINUTES**

For good reason, stir-frying has been the main way of cooking vegetables in Asia for thousands of years – preparation and cooking times are minimal but retention of nutrients and development of flavours are maximised.

1kg baby bok choy
500g choy sum
300g tat soi
1 tablespoon peanut oil
2 cloves garlic, crushed
2 teaspoons grated fresh ginger
1 tablespoon soy sauce
1 tablespoon oyster sauce

1 Slice away bottom of stems and any unsightly leaves on bok choy, choy sum and tat soi; halve bok choy lengthways.

2 Add oil to heated wok or large frying pan; stir-fry garlic and ginger until fragrant.

3 Add greens to wok; stir-fry, tossing, until just wilted.

4 Stir in sauces; toss gently until heated through.

serves 4

per serving 5.8g fat; 418kJ (100 cal)

tips Baby bok choy is sometimes called shanghai bok choy, chinese chard or white cabbage, or baby pak choi, and has a mildly acrid, appealing taste.

Choy sum is easy to identify, with its long stems and yellow flowers (hence its other common name, flowering cabbage). It is eaten stems and all.

Tat soi (also known as rosette bok choy) has a mild cabbagey, slightly bitter taste. Its flower-like leaves should be eaten soon after harvest because it gets unpleasantly strong after a few days.

cucumber and mint raita   INDIA

PREPARATION TIME **10 MINUTES (plus refrigeration time)**   COOKING TIME **2 minutes (plus cooling time)**

1 lebanese cucumber (130g)
1 teaspoon ghee
¼ teaspoon cumin seeds
¼ teaspoon brown mustard seeds
¼ teaspoon ground cumin
1 cup (280g) yogurt
1 tablespoon lemon juice
1 clove garlic, crushed
¼ teaspoon cayenne pepper
1 tablespoon chopped fresh mint

1 Peel cucumber; halve lengthways, discard seeds. Chop cucumber coarsely.

2 Heat ghee in small frying pan; cook seeds and ground cumin, stirring, until seeds pop, cool.

3 Combine spice mixture with cucumber, yogurt, juice, garlic and cayenne pepper in small bowl. Cover, refrigerate at least 2 hours.

4 Just before serving, gently stir in mint.

makes 1½ cups (400g)

per tablespoon 1g fat; 75kJ (18 cal)

tip This recipe can be made a day ahead; store, covered, in the refrigerator.

french fries FRANCE

PREPARATION TIME **15 MINUTES** COOKING TIME **20 MINUTES**

The fries can be prepared, up to the first frying, six hours ahead; re-fry before serving. We used russet burbank potatoes.

6 medium potatoes (1.2kg)
vegetable oil, for deep-frying
salt

1 Cut potatoes into 5mm slices, stack the slices then cut lengthways into 5mm strips. While still preparing potatoes, drop cut fries into a large bowl of water to prevent discolouring. Drain potatoes from water; dry well on a clean tea towel.

2 Add enough oil to come halfway up the side of a large deep saucepan. Heat oil to 150°C on a deep-frying thermometer. (If you don't have a thermometer, make sure the oil is not too hot for the first fry; you don't want potatoes to colour). Deep-fry potatoes, in small batches, until cooked through but not coloured. Drain well, then place on absorbent paper.

3 Just before serving, reheat oil for deep-frying to 180°C; deep-fry potatoes again, in batches, until crisp and golden. Drain well on plenty of crumpled absorbent paper. Sprinkle fries with salt and serve immediately.

serves 6

per serving 11.2g fat; 953kJ (228 cal)
serving suggestion Serve french fries with tomato sauce.

almond coriander couscous   MIDDLE-EAST

PREPARATION TIME **10 MINUTES (plus standing time)** COOKING TIME **10 MINUTES**

3 cups (600g) couscous
3 cups (750ml) boiling water
¼ cup (60ml) olive oil
1 clove garlic, crushed
2 green onions, chopped
¾ cup (105g) slivered almonds, toasted
⅓ cup (50g) dried currants
½ cup chopped fresh coriander

1 Combine couscous and the water in large heatproof bowl; stand, covered, 5 minutes or until water is absorbed. Fluff couscous with fork.

2 Heat oil in large frying pan, add garlic and green onion; cook, stirring, until onion is soft. Add couscous to pan, stir over heat until heated through.

3 Stir in nuts, currants and coriander.

serves 6

per serving   19.7g fat; 2416kJ (578 cal)
tip This recipe can be made three hours ahead; store, covered, in the refrigerator.

rösti

SWITZERLAND

PREPARATION TIME **20 MINUTES**   COOKING TIME **20 MINUTES**

4 medium old potatoes (800g), grated
1 medium brown onion (150g), chopped finely
60g butter, melted
¼ teaspoon cracked black peppercorns
2 tablespoons light olive oil

1 Combine potato, onion, butter and pepper in medium bowl;
mix well, drain.

2 Heat oil in large frying pan, add ⅓-cup portions of potato mixture
to pan; press into 10cm rounds. Cook until well browned on both
sides; repeat with remaining mixture.

serves 4

per serving   22g fat; 1304kJ (312 cal)
serving suggestion   Serve rösti with smoked salmon slices,
a dollop of crème fraîche and a garnish of dill.
tip   This recipe is best made close to serving.

roasted baby vegetables ITALY

PREPARATION TIME **15 MINUTES** COOKING TIME **40 MINUTES**

Eschalots are very mild, small brown onions. Baby onions, also small and brown, are sometimes called pickling onions. Both varieties are excellent when slow-roasted – with other small vegetables or on their own.

500g baby onions
250g eschalots
2 tablespoons olive oil
1kg tiny new potatoes, unpeeled
6 baby eggplants (360g),
**   halved lengthways**
250g cherry tomatoes

1 Trim off roots and remove cores of onions and eschalots; discard roots and cores.

2 Preheat oven to hot.

3 Heat oil in large flameproof baking dish; cook onions, eschalots and potatoes, stirring, until vegetables are browned all over.

4 Roast onion mixture, uncovered, in hot oven about 20 minutes or until potatoes are almost tender. Add eggplant and tomatoes to baking dish; roast, uncovered, 10 minutes or until eggplant is browned and tender.

serves 4

per serving 10.3g fat; 1317kJ (315 cal)

tips Tiny new potatoes are also known as chats; they're not a variety but an early harvest, having a thin pale skin that is easily rubbed off.
There are many different baby vegetables suitable for roasting to be found at the greengrocer's. Look for baby beetroot, turnips, carrots and so forth – they're beautifully sweet and flavoursome.

roasted tomatoes with garlic and herbs ITALY

PREPARATION TIME **10 MINUTES** COOKING TIME **1 HOUR**

9 large egg tomatoes (810g)
1 teaspoon sea salt
1 teaspoon cracked black pepper
8 sprigs fresh thyme
2 cloves garlic, sliced thinly
¼ cup (60ml) olive oil
2 teaspoons chopped fresh oregano
1 teaspoon chopped fresh thyme

1 Preheat oven to moderately hot.

2 Halve tomatoes; place cut-side up, in single layer, in large baking dish. Sprinkle tomato with combined salt, pepper, thyme sprigs and garlic; drizzle 1 tablespoon of the oil over tomato. Roast, uncovered, in moderately hot oven about 1 hour or until tomato softens and browns lightly.

3 Sprinkle tomato with combined herbs; drizzle over remaining oil.

serves 6

per serving 9.3g fat; 418kJ (100 cal)
serving suggestion These roasted tomatoes are as fantastic on a burger or in a sandwich as they are stirred through just-cooked spaghetti.
tips Roast the tomatoes in a baking dish with deep sides; this shields them from the heat, so they won't burn.
This recipe is delicious served cold or warm.

soft polenta   ITALY

PREPARATION TIME 10 MINUTES   COOKING TIME 30 MINUTES

1 litre (4 cups) milk
1 large brown onion (200g), quartered
4 bay leaves
4 cloves garlic, quartered
8 black peppercorns
1 cup (170g) instant polenta
40g butter, chopped
1 cup (80g) finely grated
**   parmesan cheese**
salt and ground black pepper

1 Combine milk, onion, bay leaves, garlic and peppercorns in large saucepan; bring to a boil. Strain milk mixture; discard solids. Return milk to same pan.

2 Gradually whisk in polenta; cook, stirring, over medium heat about 20 minutes.

3 Whisk in butter and cheese; season to taste with salt and black pepper. Serve immediately.

serves 4

per serving 25.4g fat; 2015kJ (482 cal)
tip Polenta is best made just before serving.

hash browns USA

PREPARATION TIME 10 MINUTES COOKING TIME 30 MINUTES (plus cooling time)

Ghee is butter that has been clarified to remove the milk solids and the salt; this enables ghee to be heated to a higher temperature than butter without burning.

1kg sebago potatoes, unpeeled
1 small brown onion (80g),
chopped finely
2 teaspoons finely chopped
fresh rosemary
60g ghee

1 Boil, steam or microwave potatoes in skin until just tender; drain, cool.

2 Remove skin from potatoes; cut into 1cm cubes. Combine potato, onion and rosemary in large bowl.

3 Heat ghee in medium heavy-based frying pan, place 4 egg rings in pan. Spoon ¼ cup of potato mixture into each egg ring; using spatula, spread potato mixture evenly in egg ring. Cook hash browns, pressing down frequently with spatula, until browned on both sides. Drain on absorbent paper. Repeat process with remaining potato mixture. Serve hash browns hot.

makes 12

per hash brown 5.1g fat; 418kJ (100 cal)
tips A mixture of half olive oil and half melted butter can be used instead of ghee.
Chives, thyme or parsley may be used instead of rosemary.
Other suitable varieties of potato for this recipe include desiree, ruby lou and bintje.

light meals

A quick bowl of noodles, a plate of fried rice, a wedge of quiche or frittata, or a slice of pizza fresh from the oven – all of these make great lunches, Sunday-night dinners in front of the television or just something easy after a long day's work.

combination fried rice   CHINA

PREPARATION TIME 10 MINUTES (plus refrigeration time)   COOKING TIME 10 MINUTES (plus cooling time)

You will need to cook about 1⅓ cups (260g) long-grain rice for this recipe.

2 teaspoons peanut oil
3 eggs, beaten lightly
1 tablespoon peanut oil, extra
2 cloves garlic, crushed
2 teaspoons grated fresh ginger
6 green onions, sliced thinly
4 cups cooked white long-grain rice
200g cooked shelled small prawns
200g chinese barbecued pork,
   sliced thinly
3 chinese sausages (100g),
   sliced thinly
¾ cup (90g) frozen peas, thawed
1 cup (80g) bean sprouts
2½ tablespoons light soy sauce

1 Heat half of the oil in wok or large frying pan, add half of the egg; swirl wok so egg forms an omelette over base. Cook omelette until set; remove, cool. Repeat with remaining oil and remaining egg. Roll omelettes, slice thinly.

2 Heat extra oil in same wok; stir-fry garlic, ginger and onion until fragrant. Add rice, omelette, prawns, pork, sausage, peas, sprouts and sauce; stir-fry until heated through.

serves 4

per serving 26g fat; 2604kJ (623 cal)

potato tortilla

SPAIN

PREPARATION TIME **10 MINUTES**
(plus standing time)
COOKING TIME **50 MINUTES**

This Spanish tortilla (or omelette) can be
made several hours ahead.

4 medium potatoes (800g)
1 large brown onion (200g),
   sliced thinly
olive oil, for shallow-frying
2 medium red capsicums (400g)
6 eggs, beaten lightly
2 teaspoons sea salt

1 Peel potatoes and slice thinly, ensuring
they are sliced evenly; pat dry with
absorbent paper. Shallow-fry potato and
onion in hot oil, in batches, until browned
lightly; drain on absorbent paper.

2 Quarter capsicums, remove and discard
seeds and membranes. Roast under
a grill or in a very hot oven, skin-side up,
until skin blisters and blackens. Cover
capsicum pieces with plastic or paper
for 5 minutes, peel away skin; slice
capsicum thinly.

3 Combine potato, onion, capsicum,
egg and salt in a large bowl.

4 Heat oiled 26cm non-stick frying pan;
pour in potato mixture, press down firmly.
Cook, uncovered, over low heat about
8 minutes or until the base of the tortilla
is browned.

5 Cover the pan handle with foil and
place the tortilla under a hot grill until
browned and set.

6 Invert onto board or serving plate and
stand for 10 minutes before cutting
into wedges.

serves 4

per serving 30.6g fat; 1860kJ (445 cal)

quiche lorraine   FRANCE

PREPARATION TIME **30 MINUTES (plus refrigeration and standing time)**   COOKING TIME **1 HOUR (plus cooling time)**

Quiche lorraine is a savoury flan which originated in the area of Lorraine in France. The pastry case can be "baked blind", cooled and stored in an airtight container for about a week. If the weather is humid, store it in the refrigerator.

1¾ cups (255g) plain flour
150g cold butter, chopped
1 egg yolk
2 teaspoons lemon juice, approximately
⅓ cup (80ml) cold water
1 medium brown onion (150g), chopped finely
3 bacon rashers, chopped
3 eggs
300ml cream
½ cup (125ml) milk
¾ cup (120g) grated cheddar cheese

1 Sift flour into bowl; rub in butter. Add egg yolk, juice and enough water to make ingredients cling together. Knead gently on lightly floured surface until smooth, cover; refrigerate 30 minutes.

2 Roll pastry so it is large enough to line a deep 23cm loose-base flan tin. If weather is hot and pastry is difficult to handle, roll pastry between two pieces of plastic wrap or greaseproof or baking paper. Lift pastry into flan tin, gently ease pastry into side of tin; do not stretch pastry or it will shrink during the cooking.

3 Use the rolling pin to trim the edges of pastry neatly. Place flan on oven tray for easier handling. Preheat oven to moderately hot.

4 Cover pastry with greaseproof or baking paper, fill with dried beans or rice. This is called "baking blind". Bake in moderately hot oven for 10 minutes; remove paper and beans carefully. Bake pastry about 10 minutes or until golden brown; cool to room temperature. Reduce oven temperature to moderate. Cool the beans or rice; store in an airtight container for future use when baking blind.

5 Cook onion and bacon in lightly oiled small frying pan until onion is soft; drain away excess fat, cool before spreading into pastry case.

6 Using whisk, beat eggs in medium bowl; add cream, milk and cheese. Whisk until just combined; pour into pastry case. Bake in moderate oven about 35 minutes or until filling is set and brown.

7 Stand quiche 5 minutes before removing from tin.

serves 6

per serving 53.3g fat; 2889kJ (690 cal)
serving suggestion Serve a small wedge of quiche with a light salad for a first course. It can be served warm, hot or cold.

frittata with onions and zucchini ITALY

PREPARATION TIME 20 MINUTES COOKING TIME 30 MINUTES (plus cooling time)

20g butter, melted
2 tablespoons olive oil
2 medium white onions (300g),
   sliced thinly
6 eggs, beaten lightly
¾ cup (60g) grated parmesan cheese
1 small zucchini (90g), sliced thinly
1 tablespoon shredded fresh basil

1 Preheat oven to moderate. Brush base and sides of deep 19cm-square cake pan with butter. Heat oil in medium frying pan. Cook onion, stirring, until soft; cool.

2 Combine onion, egg, cheese, zucchini and basil in medium bowl; mix well. Pour mixture into prepared pan. Bake in moderate oven about 25 minutes or until browned lightly and set.

serves 6

per serving 17.4g fat; 894kJ (214 cal)
tip This recipe can be made a day ahead; store, covered, in the refrigerator.

singapore noodles

SINGAPORE

PREPARATION TIME **30 MINUTES** COOKING TIME **15 MINUTES**

250g dried thin egg noodles
2 tablespoons peanut oil
4 eggs, beaten lightly
3 cloves garlic, crushed
1 tablespoon grated fresh ginger
1 medium white onion (150g), sliced thinly
2 tablespoons mild curry paste
230g can water chestnuts, drained, chopped coarsely
3 green onions, chopped diagonally
200g chinese barbecued pork, sliced
500g medium uncooked prawns, shelled, deveined
2 tablespoons light soy sauce
2 tablespoons oyster sauce

1 Cook noodles in large saucepan of boiling water, uncovered, until just tender; drain.

2 Meanwhile, heat half of the oil in hot wok or large frying pan; add half of the egg, swirl wok to make a thin omelette. Remove omelette from wok; roll omelette, cut into thin strips. Repeat with remaining egg.

3 Heat remaining oil in wok; stir-fry garlic and ginger 1 minute. Add white onion and paste; stir-fry 2 minutes or until fragrant.

4 Add water chestnuts, green onion and pork; stir-fry about 2 minutes or until chestnuts are browned lightly.

5 Add prawns; stir-fry until prawns are just changed in colour. Add noodles, combined sauces and omelette; stir-fry, tossing, until sauce thickens and noodles are heated through.

serves 4

per serving 27.2g fat; 2658kJ (636 cal)

tips You can buy ready-to-eat barbecued pork at specialist Chinese barbecue shops.
Have all the ingredients for this recipe chopped and ready to go, so that they can be stir-fried in just a few minutes and eaten immediately – the noodles become unappetising and gluey after being mixed with the other ingredients if the finished dish sits for any length of time after the wok comes off the heat.

pissaladière FRANCE

PREPARATION TIME **25 MINUTES** COOKING TIME **1 HOUR 10 MINUTES**

Pissaladière is traditionally made with a yeast dough, similar to pizza, or sometimes flaky pastry. We have used a simple dough. The onion mixture can be made a day ahead. The recipe is best cooked just before serving.

50g butter
1 tablespoon olive oil
3 large brown onions (600g),
  sliced thinly
2 cloves garlic, crushed
1 bay leaf
1 sprig fresh thyme
1 tablespoon drained baby capers
¾ cup (110g) self-raising flour
¾ cup (110g) plain flour
30g butter, chopped, extra
¾ cup (180ml) buttermilk
20 drained anchovy fillets,
  approximately, halved lengthways
½ cup (90g) small black olives

1 Heat butter and oil in large saucepan; cook onion, garlic, bay leaf and thyme, covered, stirring occasionally, over low heat about 30 minutes or until onion is very soft but not browned. Cook, uncovered, 10 minutes. Remove bay leaf and thyme sprig; stir in capers.

2 Preheat oven to moderately hot.

3 Meanwhile, sift flours into large bowl. Rub in extra butter; stir in buttermilk to form a soft dough. Turn dough onto lightly floured surface; knead until smooth.

4 Roll out dough to form a rough rectangular shape, about 25cm x 35cm. Place on a greased oven tray.

5 Spread onion mixture over dough, spreading it to edges. Top with anchovy and olives in a diamond pattern. Bake in moderately hot oven about 30 minutes or until base is browned and crisp.

serves 6

per serving 16.4g fat; 1371kJ (328 cal)

pizza ITALY

PREPARATION TIME 30 MINUTES (plus standing time)   COOKING TIME 35 MINUTES (plus cooling time)

2 teaspoons olive oil

**1 medium brown onion (150g),
chopped finely**

1 clove garlic, crushed

400g can tomatoes

1 tablespoon tomato paste

**2 teaspoons finely chopped
fresh oregano**

1 teaspoon sugar

**1¼ cups (125g) grated
mozzarella cheese**

2 tablespoons grated parmesan cheese

45g can anchovy fillets, drained

**1 small red capsicum (150g),
sliced thinly**

3 button mushrooms, sliced thinly

½ cup (60g) black olives

¼ cup fresh basil leaves

DOUGH

15g compressed yeast

½ teaspoon sugar

½ cup (125ml) lukewarm water

1½ cups (225g) plain flour

pinch salt

2 tablespoons olive oil

1 Heat oil in large saucepan; cook onion until soft. Add garlic; cook, stirring, 1 minute. Add undrained crushed tomatoes, paste, oregano and sugar; bring to a boil. Reduce heat; simmer, uncovered, stirring occasionally, about 10 minutes or until sauce is thick and smooth; cool.

2 Preheat oven to hot. Flatten dough into circle about 2.5cm thick. Roll out, from centre to edge, to fit 25cm pizza pan. Spread cooled sauce over dough base of pizza.

3 Combine cheeses in small bowl; sprinkle half of the cheese mixture over pizza. Top with anchovies, capsicum and mushrooms. Sprinkle with olives and remaining cheese. Bake in hot oven about 15 minutes or until crust is golden brown. Sprinkle with basil to serve.

dough Combine yeast with sugar in small bowl; add the water. Let stand about 10 minutes or until bubbles appear on surface. Combine flour and salt in medium bowl; make well in centre. Add oil and yeast mixture; mix to a firm dough by hand. Turn dough onto floured surface; knead about 10 minutes or until dough is smooth and elastic. Place dough in lightly oiled medium bowl. Cover; stand in warm place about 30 minutes or until dough has doubled in bulk. Knock dough down; knead into smooth ball.

serves 4

per serving 21.3g fat; 2048kJ (490 cal)

tip The pizza can be prepared and frozen in its unbaked form. Place frozen pizza in hot oven; allow about 10 minutes extra cooking time.

macaroni cheese   ENGLAND

PREPARATION TIME **10 MINUTES**   COOKING TIME **50 MINUTES (plus cooling time)**

This recipe can be prepared several hours ahead; reheat before serving.

300g macaroni
4 bacon rashers (280g), chopped
50g butter
⅓ cup (50g) plain flour
1 litre (4 cups) milk
1 cup (125g) coarsely grated
cheddar cheese
½ cup (40g) finely grated
pecorino cheese
2 tablespoons wholegrain mustard
½ cup (35g) stale breadcrumbs
20g butter, chopped, extra

1 Cook pasta in large saucepan of boiling water, uncovered, until just tender; drain.

2 Preheat oven to moderately hot.

3 Meanwhile, cook bacon in medium frying pan, stirring, until bacon is crisp; drain on absorbent paper.

4 Melt butter in same pan, add flour; cook, stirring, 1 minute. Gradually stir in milk; continue stirring until sauce boils and thickens. Cool for 2 minutes, then stir in cheeses and mustard.

5 Combine pasta, sauce and bacon in large bowl; transfer mixture to oiled deep 2-litre (8 cup) ovenproof dish. Top with breadcrumbs, dot with extra butter.

6 Bake, uncovered, in moderately hot oven about 30 minutes or until top is browned.

serves 4

per serving 44.2g fat; 3644kJ (870 cal)

tip You can substitute cheeses of your choice, such as gruyère, parmesan, swiss or romano.

spaghetti puttanesca   ITALY

PREPARATION TIME 15 MINUTES   COOKING TIME 15 MINUTES

375g spaghetti
¼ cup (60ml) olive oil
2 cloves garlic, crushed
4 medium tomatoes (760g),
   chopped coarsely
½ cup chopped fresh flat-leaf parsley
12 stuffed green olives, sliced thinly
45g can anchovy fillets, chopped finely
1 tablespoon shredded fresh basil
pinch chilli powder

1 Cook pasta in large saucepan of boiling water until tender; drain.

2 Meanwhile, heat oil in medium frying pan; cook garlic until it just changes colour. Add remaining ingredients; cook, stirring, 5 minutes. Combine sauce and pasta.

serves 4

per serving 16.6g fat; 2027kJ (485 cal)

tip The puttanesca sauce can be made two days ahead; store, covered, in the refrigerator.

desserts

Few people, no matter their nationality, can resist the sweet and luscious allure of cakes, flans, gelato, pies, puddings and tarts. A mouth-watering array of recipes fills this chapter – some are undeniably wicked, some only pleasingly naughty – and all are tempting in the extreme.

sticky date pudding with butterscotch sauce   ENGLAND

PREPARATION TIME 10 MINUTES (plus standing time)   COOKING TIME 1 HOUR (plus standing time)

1¼ cups (200g) seeded dried dates
1¼ cups (310ml) boiling water
1 teaspoon bicarbonate of soda
50g butter, chopped
½ cup (100g) firmly packed
**   brown sugar**
2 eggs, beaten lightly
1 cup (150g) self-raising flour

BUTTERSCOTCH SAUCE
¾ cup (150g) firmly packed
**   brown sugar**
300ml cream
80g butter

1 Preheat oven to moderate. Grease deep 20cm-round cake pan; line base
with baking paper.

2 Combine dates and the water in medium heatproof bowl. Stir in soda; stand 5 minutes.

3 Blend or process date mixture with butter and sugar until pureed. Add eggs and flour;
blend or process until just combined. Pour mixture into prepared pan.

4 Bake, uncovered, in moderate oven about 1 hour (cover with foil if pudding starts
to overbrown). Stand 10 minutes; turn onto serving plate. Serve warm with
butterscotch sauce.

butterscotch sauce Combine ingredients in medium saucepan; stir over
low heat until sauce is smooth and slightly thickened.

serves 6

per serving 38.4g fat; 2867kJ (686 cal)

tips Both the pudding and sauce can be made a day ahead; store separately,
covered, in the refrigerator.
You can freeze the pudding for up to three months. Defrost and warm in the
microwave oven while making the butterscotch sauce.

serving suggestion This pudding is good served warm with sliced fresh
strawberries and thickened cream.

flourless hazelnut chocolate cake   FRANCE

PREPARATION TIME **20 MINUTES**   COOKING TIME **1 HOUR** (plus cooling time)

Hazelnut meal replaces the flour in this recipe. Hazelnut meal, also sold as ground hazelnuts, is a flour-like substance made after the nuts have been roasted.

⅓ cup (35g) cocoa powder
⅓ cup (80ml) hot water
150g dark eating chocolate, melted
150g butter, melted
1⅓ cups (275g) firmly packed
  brown sugar
1 cup (125g) hazelnut meal
4 eggs, separated
1 tablespoon cocoa powder, extra

1 Preheat oven to moderate. Grease deep 19cm-square cake pan; line base and sides with baking paper.

2 Blend cocoa with the water in large bowl until smooth. Stir in chocolate, butter, sugar, hazelnut meal and egg yolks.

3 Beat egg whites in small bowl with electric mixer until soft peaks form; fold into chocolate mixture in two batches.

4 Pour mixture into prepared pan; bake in moderate oven about 1 hour or until firm. Stand cake 15 minutes; turn onto wire rack, top-side up, to cool. Dust with sifted extra cocoa to serve.

serves 8

per serving 34g fat; 1768kJ (423 cal)
tip The cake can be made up to four days ahead; store, covered, in the refrigerator. It can also be frozen for up to three months.

cassata

ITALY

PREPARATION TIME **1 HOUR** (plus freezing time)

2 eggs, separated
½ cup (110g) icing sugar mixture
½ cup (125ml) cream
few drops almond essence

SECOND LAYER
2 eggs, separated
½ cup (110g) icing sugar mixture
½ cup (125ml) cream
60g dark eating chocolate, melted
2 tablespoons cocoa powder
1½ tablespoons water

THIRD LAYER
1 cup (250ml) cream
1 teaspoon vanilla essence
1 egg white, beaten lightly
⅓ cup (55g) icing sugar mixture
2 tablespoons red glacé cherries, chopped finely
2 glacé apricots, chopped finely
2 glacé pineapple rings, chopped finely
1 tablespoon green glacé cherries, chopped finely
30g flaked almonds, toasted

1 Beat egg whites in small bowl with electric mixer until firm peaks form; gradually beat in icing sugar. Fold in lightly beaten egg yolks.

2 Beat cream and almond essence in small bowl with electric mixer until soft peaks form; fold into egg mixture. Pour mixture into deep 20cm-round cake pan. Level top; freeze until firm.

3 Spread second layer over almond layer; freeze until firm.

4 Spread third layer over second layer; freeze until firm.

5 Run small spatula around edge of cassata; wipe hot cloth over base and side of pan. Turn cassata out onto serving plate.

second layer Beat egg whites in small bowl with electric mixer until firm peaks form; gradually beat in sifted icing sugar. Beat cream in small bowl until soft peaks form; fold in egg white mixture. Place chocolate in small bowl; stir in egg yolks. Stir combined cocoa and water into chocolate mixture; stir chocolate mixture through cream mixture.

third layer Beat cream and vanilla essence in small bowl with electric mixer until firm peaks form. Beat egg white in small bowl with electric mixer until soft peaks form; gradually add icing sugar to egg white, beating well after each addition. Stir egg white mixture into cream; stir in fruit and almonds.

serves 8

per serving 30.5g fat; 2069kJ (495 cal)

lemon gelato   ITALY

PREPARATION TIME **15 MINUTES (plus freezing time)**   COOKING TIME **15 MINUTES (plus cooling time)**

½ cup (110g) caster sugar
½ cup (125ml) water
**½ cup (125ml) sweet or dry
    white wine**
**½ cup (125ml) lemon
    juice, strained**
1 egg white

1   Combine sugar, the water and wine in small saucepan; stir over
    low heat until sugar dissolves. Bring to a boil; reduce heat. Simmer,
    uncovered, 10 minutes; cool.

2   Stir juice into mixture; mix well. Pour mixture into medium shallow pan;
    freeze about 1 hour or until mixture is just firm.

3   Remove from freezer. Turn mixture into medium bowl; using fork,
    beat until smooth. Beat egg white in small bowl with electric mixer
    until firm; fold into lemon mixture. Return to pan; freeze until firm.

serves 2

per serving   0.1g fat; 1158kJ (277 cal)

mini apple charlottes with caramel sauce ENGLAND

PREPARATION TIME **25 MINUTES** COOKING TIME **30 MINUTES**

We used Granny Smith apples here, but another variety, such as Golden Delicious, is an acceptable substitute.

4 large apples (800g)
¼ cup (50g) firmly packed brown sugar
¼ cup (60ml) orange juice
1 loaf sliced raisin bread (560g)
80g butter, melted

CARAMEL SAUCE
50g butter
½ cup (100g) firmly packed brown sugar
⅓ cup (80ml) orange juice

1 Grease four 1-cup (250ml) metal moulds.

2 Peel and core apples; cut into thin wedges. Cook apple with sugar and juice in large frying pan, stirring until apple browns and mixture bubbles and thickens.

3 Preheat oven to hot.

4 Remove crusts from bread slices. Cut one 5.5cm round from each of four bread slices; cut remaining bread slices into three strips each. Brush one side of each round and strip with butter. Place one round, buttered-side down, in each mould; line side of each mould with bread strips, buttered-side against side of mould, slightly overlapping edges. Firmly pack warm apple mixture into moulds. Fold end of each bread strip down into centre of charlotte to enclose filling; press firmly to seal.

5 Place moulds on oven tray; bake, uncovered, in hot oven about 15 minutes or until charlottes are golden brown. Turn, top-side up, onto serving plates; drizzle with caramel sauce.

caramel sauce Melt butter in small frying pan. Add sugar; stir until dissolved. Add juice; cook, stirring, until sauce thickens slightly.

serves 4

per serving 31.6g fat; 3515kJ (841 cal)
tips It's best if you use sliced raisin bread that's a few days old. You can also use plain white bread instead of the raisin bread.

boiled christmas pudding

ENGLAND

PREPARATION TIME 30 MINUTES
(plus standing time)
COOKING TIME 6 HOURS
(plus cooling time)

1½ cups (250g) raisins, chopped
1½ cups (250g) sultanas
1 cup (185g) currants
¾ cup (185g) mixed peel
1 teaspoon grated lemon rind
2 tablespoons lemon juice
2 tablespoons brandy
250g butter
2 cups (500g) firmly packed
**   brown sugar**
5 eggs
1¼ cups (200g) plain flour
½ teaspoon ground nutmeg
½ teaspoon mixed spice
4 cups (280g) stale breadcrumbs,
**   lightly packed**

1 Combine fruit, rind, juice and brandy in large bowl, mix well. Cover, stand overnight or up to a week.

2 Beat butter and sugar in large bowl with electric mixer only until combined. Beat in eggs, one at a time, only until combined between each addition. Add creamed mixture to fruit mixture; add sifted dry ingredients and breadcrumbs, mix well.

3 Have ready a large boiler three-quarters full of rapidly boiling water, 2.5m of kitchen string and ½ cup (75g) extra plain flour.

4 Wearing thick rubber gloves, dip prepared pudding cloth into boiling water, boil 1 minute. Squeeze excess water from cloth.

5 Working quickly, spread hot cloth on bench. Rub extra flour into centre of cloth to cover an area about 40cm in diameter, leaving flour thicker in the centre where the "skin" will need to be thickest.

6 Place cloth into medium bowl then place pudding mixture in centre; gather cloth evenly around pudding. Lift pudding out of bowl, pat into a round shape. Tie cloth tightly with string as close to mixture as possible. Tie a loop in string to make pudding easy to handle. Pull ends tightly to make pudding as round as possible.

7 Gently lower pudding into boiling water; cover with tight-fitting lid, boil rapidly for 6 hours. Replenish with boiling water as required.

8 Place handle of wooden spoon through loop of string, lift from water. Suspend pudding from spoon by placing spoon over rungs of an upturned stool or wedging a handle in a drawer; pudding should swing freely. Twist wet ends of cloth around supporting string, away from pudding.

9 Hang pudding 10 minutes or until cloth is dry around pudding. Place pudding in a medium bowl, cut string, carefully peel back cloth a little. Invert pudding onto a plate, carefully pull back cloth completely; cool. Wrap pudding in plastic wrap, seal tightly in freezer bag or airtight container; refrigerate or freeze.

10 To reheat pudding, remove plastic wrap; wrap clean dry unfloured cloth around pudding. Boil 2 hours following cooking instructions in step 7; remove from cloth. Stand pudding 20 minutes for skin to darken.

serves 10

per serving 24.9g fat; 3248kJ (777 cal)
serving suggestion Serve with vanilla custard and berries.
tip The pudding can also be reheated in the microwave oven; reheat 4 single serves at a time.

lemon delicious ENGLAND

PREPARATION TIME 20 MINUTES COOKING TIME 45 MINUTES

This English pudding is more traditionally known as baked lemon pudding. Interestingly though, and probably as a time-honoured mark of affection, this dish is best known in Australia as lemon delicious.

3 eggs, separated
½ cup (110g) caster sugar
30g butter, melted
¾ cup (180ml) milk
2 teaspoons grated lemon rind
⅓ cup (80ml) lemon juice
½ cup (75g) self-raising flour
¼ cup (55g) caster sugar, extra

1 Beat egg yolks and sugar in small bowl with electric mixer until thick and creamy; transfer to large bowl. Stir in butter, milk, rind, juice and sifted flour.

2 Beat egg whites in small bowl with electric mixer until soft peaks form; add extra sugar gradually, beating until dissolved after additions. Fold into lemon mixture in two batches.

3 Pour mixture into lightly greased 1-litre (4 cup) ovenproof dish, or four individual 1-cup (250ml) dishes. Place in baking dish with enough hot water to come halfway up side of dish, or dishes.

4 Bake in moderate oven about 45 minutes (25 minutes for individual dishes) or until pudding is set.

serves 4

per serving 12.4g fat; 1553kJ (371 cal)

chocolate mousse

FRANCE

PREPARATION TIME **15 MINUTES**
(plus refrigeration time)
COOKING TIME **5 MINUTES**
(plus cooling time)

200g dark eating chocolate
300ml thickened cream
3 eggs, separated
2 tablespoons caster sugar

1 Break off and reserve a long piece of the chocolate, weighing about 25g, for making decorative chocolate shavings.

2 Chop remaining chocolate coarsely then combine it with half of the cream in large heatproof bowl. Place bowl over saucepan of simmering water; stir until chocolate has melted. Cool chocolate mixture for 5 minutes then stir in egg yolks, one at a time.

3 Beat egg whites in small bowl on highest speed with electric mixer until soft peaks form; add sugar, beat until dissolved. Gently fold whites, in two batches, into chocolate mixture; pour mixture into four ⅔-cup (160ml) serving glasses. Refrigerate 3 hours or overnight.

4 Whip remaining cream until soft peaks form. Make chocolate shavings by running a vegetable peeler along one edge of the reserved piece of chocolate. Dollop cream and sprinkle chocolate over each mousse.

serves 4

per serving 46.1g fat; 2567kJ (614 cal)

tips When the egg yolks are stirred into the melted chocolate mixture, work quickly and stir rapidly to avoid the yolks "scrambling" in the still-warm mixture.
When melting chocolate, take care that it does not come into contact with water. If it does, it will "seize", that is, become lumpy and lose its sheen. If this occurs, you'll have to start over with a new piece of chocolate.

pavlova

AUSTRALIA

PREPARATION TIME **15 MINUTES**
COOKING TIME **1 HOUR 15 MINUTES (plus cooling time)**

Pavlova is said to have been invented by Perth chef
Bert Sachse in the 1930s. It was so named because it was
considered to be as light as the dancer Anna Pavlova.

4 egg whites
1 cup (220g) caster sugar
1 tablespoon cornflour
1 teaspoon white vinegar
300ml thickened cream
2 teaspoons vanilla essence
1 tablespoon icing sugar

1   Cover oven tray with baking paper; mark 18cm circle
    on baking paper.

2   Beat egg whites in small bowl with electric mixer until
    soft peaks form; gradually add caster sugar, beating
    until dissolved after each addition. Fold in cornflour
    and vinegar. Preheat oven to very slow.

3   Spread meringue inside circle on prepared tray. For best
    results, do not squash or flatten mixture but shape side
    up and in towards the centre, like a mound. Make furrows
    up side of meringue using spatula, level top.

4   Bake meringue in very slow oven about 1¼ hours
    or until dry. Turn oven off; leave meringue to cool in
    oven with door ajar.

5   An hour before serving, beat cream, essence and sifted
    icing sugar in medium bowl with electric mixer until soft
    peaks form. Fill meringue with cream mixture, decorate
    with fruit of your choice.

serves 8

per serving   13.8g fat; 1076kJ (257 cal)
tip   The meringue case can be made four days ahead
and stored in an airtight container.

panna cotta ITALY

PREPARATION TIME 20 MINUTES (plus refrigeration time) COOKING TIME 5 MINUTES

300ml thickened cream
1 cup (250ml) milk
⅓ cup (75g) caster sugar
2 teaspoons vanilla essence
2½ teaspoons gelatine
1 tablespoon water
250g strawberries, halved
¼ cup (60ml) orange juice
2 teaspoons icing sugar mixture

1 Grease six ½-cup (125ml) moulds.

2 Combine cream, milk and sugar in small saucepan; stir over low heat until sugar is dissolved. Stir in vanilla essence.

3 Sprinkle gelatine over the water in a cup, stand cup in pan of simmering water; stir until gelatine is dissolved.

4 Stir gelatine mixture into cream mixture. Pour evenly into prepared moulds, cover; refrigerate about 6 hours or until set.

5 Meanwhile, combine strawberries, juice and icing sugar in medium bowl, cover; refrigerate 1 hour.

6 Just before serving, turn panna cotta onto serving plates and serve with the strawberry mixture.

serves 6

per serving 20.1g fat; 1124kJ (269 cal)
serving suggestion Panna cotta is a light, silky-smooth "custard".
It can be served with seasonal fruit of your choice.
tip This recipe can be made a day ahead; store, covered, in the refrigerator.

crème brûlée FRANCE

PREPARATION TIME **15 MINUTES (plus refrigeration time)** COOKING TIME **40 MINUTES (plus cooling time)**

There's something very seductive about the silky texture of a perfectly made crème brûlée; translated, its name means "burnt cream". This is a divine dessert that combines smooth, rich vanilla custard and crunchy toffee in every mouthful.

1 vanilla bean
3 cups (750ml) thickened cream
6 egg yolks
¼ cup (55g) caster sugar
⅓ cup (55g) pure icing sugar,
**   approximately**

1 Preheat oven to moderately slow.

2 Split vanilla bean in half lengthways then, using a sharp knife, scrape seeds from bean; reserve seeds. Combine bean and cream in medium saucepan; heat until just below boiling point.

3 Meanwhile, whisk egg yolks, caster sugar and vanilla seeds in medium heatproof bowl; gradually whisk in the hot cream mixture. Place the bowl over a saucepan of simmering water – do not have the water touching the base of the bowl. Stir over heat for about 10 minutes or until mixture thickens slightly and coats the back of a spoon.

4 Remove the bean – it can be washed, dried and kept for another use.
Place six ½-cup (125ml) ovenproof dishes in a baking dish, pour the cream mixture into the ovenproof dishes level with the top, as they will shrink slightly. Add enough boiling water to come three-quarters of the way up the side of the dishes. Bake in moderately slow oven about 20 minutes or until custard is just set. Remove dishes from the water; cool to room temperature. Cover; refrigerate several hours or overnight.

5 Place dishes in shallow baking dish filled with ice-cubes (the ice helps to keep custard firm while grilling). Sprinkle each custard evenly with about 1 heaped teaspoon of sifted icing sugar; wipe clean the edges of the dishes. Place under a hot grill until the sugar is just melted, not coloured. Sprinkle custards with second layer of sifted icing sugar; place under hot grill until sugar is golden brown.

serves 6

per serving 24g fat; 1279kJ (306 cal)
tips This recipe can be prepared a day ahead; grill the tops of custards up to an hour before serving.
Alternatively, use a small blow torch to melt and caramelise the sugar. Small blow torches are available from hardware stores, some kitchenware shops and professional cookware outlets.

bread and butter pudding
ENGLAND

PREPARATION TIME 20 MINUTES (plus standing time)   COOKING TIME 50 MINUTES

6 thin slices white bread
40g butter, softened
4 eggs
⅓ cup (75g) caster sugar
3½ cups (875ml) milk
1 teaspoon vanilla essence
½ cup (80g) sultanas
ground nutmeg or ground cinnamon

1 Trim crusts from bread, butter each slice; cut each slice into four triangles. Arrange two rows of triangles, butter-side up, overlapping slightly, along base of shallow 2-litre (8 cup) ovenproof dish. Centre another row of triangles over first two rows, with triangles facing in opposite direction to triangles in first layer.

2 Whisk eggs, sugar, milk and essence together in bowl.

3 Preheat oven to moderately slow. Pour half of the custard mixture over bread; stand 10 minutes.

4 Whisk remaining custard mixture again, add sultanas; pour into dish. Sprinkle with nutmeg or cinnamon. Stand dish in larger baking dish, with enough boiling water to come halfway up side of dish.

5 Bake, uncovered, in moderately slow oven about 50 minutes or until custard is set.

serves 4

per serving 23.6g fat; 2244kJ (536 cal)
serving suggestion Serve this pudding hot or cold, with stewed fruit and ice-cream.
tips This recipe can be made a day ahead; store, covered, in the refrigerator.
Substitute any dried fruit of your choice in this recipe.

pumpkin pie USA

PREPARATION TIME **30 MINUTES** (plus refrigeration time) COOKING TIME **1 HOUR 10 MINUTES** (plus cooling time)

Perhaps the most well-known pumpkin recipe comes from the United States, in the form of this delicious pie. You will need to cook about 350g pumpkin for this recipe.

1 cup (150g) plain flour
¼ cup (35g) self-raising flour
2 tablespoons cornflour
2 tablespoons icing sugar mixture
125g cold butter, chopped
2 tablespoons cold water,
 approximately

FILLING
2 eggs
¼ cup (50g) firmly packed brown sugar
2 tablespoons maple syrup
1 cup cooked mashed pumpkin
⅔ cup (160ml) evaporated milk
1 teaspoon ground cinnamon
½ teaspoon ground nutmeg
pinch ground allspice

1 Sift flours and sugar into medium bowl, rub in butter. Add enough water to make ingredients cling together. Press dough into a ball, knead gently on floured surface until smooth; cover, refrigerate 30 minutes.

2 Preheat oven to moderately hot. Roll dough on floured surface until large enough to line 23cm pie plate. Lift pastry into pie plate, ease into side; trim edge. Use scraps of pastry to make a double edge of pastry; trim and decorate edge.

3 Place pie plate on oven tray, line pastry with baking paper, fill with dried beans or rice. Bake in moderately hot oven 10 minutes. Remove paper and beans; bake 10 minutes or until lightly browned, cool. Reduce oven temperature to moderate.

4 Pour filling into pastry case; bake in moderate oven about 50 minutes or until filling is set, cool. Lightly dust with extra sifted icing sugar, if desired.

filling Beat eggs, sugar and maple syrup in small bowl with electric mixer until thick. Stir in pumpkin, milk and spices.

serves 6

per serving 22.1g fat; 1843kJ (441 cal)
tip This pie can be made a day ahead; store, covered, in the refrigerator.

tarte tatin FRANCE

PREPARATION TIME 30 MINUTES (plus refrigeration time)   COOKING TIME 45 MINUTES (plus cooling and standing time)

Golden delicious apples will give you the best results in this recipe.

2 tablespoons orange juice
⅔ cup (150g) caster sugar
70g butter
3 medium apples (450g), peeled

PASTRY
1 cup (150g) plain flour
80g cold butter, chopped
1 tablespoon caster sugar
1 tablespoon cold water, approximately

1 Combine juice, sugar and butter in 23cm heavy-based ovenproof frying pan; stir over heat, without boiling, until sugar is dissolved. Simmer, stirring occasionally, until mixture becomes a thick, light golden caramel. Remove from heat.

2 Halve apples; cut each half into 3 wedges, remove cores. Pack apple wedges tightly into pan over caramel, return to heat; simmer, uncovered, about 15 minutes or until most of the liquid is evaporated and caramel is dark golden brown. Remove from heat; cool 1 hour. Preheat oven to moderate.

3 Roll pastry into circle a little larger than the pan. Lift pastry, without stretching it, on top of apples, tuck inside edge of pan. Bake in moderate oven about 25 minutes or until pastry is golden brown and crisp. Remove tarte from oven, stand 5 minutes. Carefully invert tarte onto plate. Serve warm with cream, if desired.

pastry   Blend or process flour, butter and sugar until mixture resembles fine breadcrumbs. Add just enough water to make ingredients just cling together. Knead dough on floured surface until smooth. Cover, refrigerate 1 hour.

serves 6

per serving 21.2g fat; 1693kJ (405 cal)

tip Apple caramel mixture and pastry can be made a day ahead; store separately, covered, in the refrigerator.

fruit flan

FRANCE

PREPARATION TIME 45 MINUTES (plus refrigeration time)
COOKING TIME 30 MINUTES (plus cooling time)

This fruit flan is at its best eaten on the day it is made.

1 cup (150g) plain flour
1 tablespoon icing sugar mixture
90g cold butter, chopped
1 egg yolk
1 tablespoon lemon juice, approximately
½ x 425g can apricot halves
250g strawberries
1 medium kiwi fruit (85g), sliced
1 tablespoon arrowroot
1 tablespoon brandy

CREME PATISSIERE
1¼ cups (310ml) milk
1 egg
2 egg yolks
1 tablespoon plain flour
2 tablespoons cornflour
¼ cup (55g) caster sugar
1 teaspoon vanilla essence
50g butter, chopped

1 Sift flour and sugar into large bowl, rub in butter. Add egg yolk and enough lemon juice to mix to a firm dough. Press ingredients together into a smooth ball, cover; refrigerate 30 minutes. Roll pastry on lightly floured surface or between pieces of plastic wrap or greaseproof paper until large enough to line 24cm-round loose-base flan tin. Ease pastry gently into side of tin with fingers. Roll rolling pin over top of tin to cut off excess pastry, refrigerate 20 minutes. Preheat oven to moderately hot. Cover pastry case with greaseproof paper, fill with dried beans or rice. Bake in moderately hot oven for 7 minutes, remove paper and beans; bake 7 minutes or until lightly browned, cool to room temperature.

2 Spread crème pâtissière into pastry case.

3 Drain apricots, slice; reserve syrup. Arrange apricot, strawberries and kiwi fruit decoratively over crème. Blend arrowroot with about 2 tablespoons of the reserved syrup in small saucepan; stir in brandy and remaining syrup. Stir constantly over heat until mixture boils and thickens. Brush glaze over fruit; refrigerate flan several hours before serving.

crème pâtissière Blend or process ¼ cup (60ml) of the milk, egg, egg yolks, flours and sugar until combined. Place remaining milk in small saucepan; bring to a boil. Pour hot milk gradually into blender or processor while motor is operating; blend or process until smooth. Return mixture to saucepan; stir constantly over heat until mixture boils and thickens. Remove from heat, stir in essence and butter until butter is melted; cool to room temperature.

serves 6

per serving 25.3g fat; 1833kJ (438 cal)
tips The pastry case can be made a day ahead; store in an airtight container. The baked unfilled pastry case can be frozen for up to two months.
Uncooked rice or dried beans used to weigh down the pastry are not suitable for eating. Use them every time you bake-blind; store in an airtight storage jar.

profiteroles   FRANCE

Profiteroles can be prepared a day ahead. Fill the choux puffs close to serving and reheat the chocolate sauce.

75g butter, chopped
½ teaspoon salt
¾ cup (180ml) water
¾ cup (110g) plain flour
4 eggs

CREME PATISSIERE
2¼ cups (560ml) milk
1 vanilla bean
6 egg yolks
⅔ cup (150g) caster sugar
½ cup (75g) plain flour

CHOCOLATE LIQUEUR SAUCE
100g dark eating chocolate, chopped
30g butter, chopped
⅓ cup (80ml) cream
1 tablespoon Grand Marnier
**   or Cointreau**

1 Preheat oven to moderately hot.

2 Combine butter, salt and the water in medium saucepan; bring to a boil, stirring, until butter is melted. Add sifted flour and stir vigorously over heat until mixture leaves side of pan and forms a smooth ball.

3 Transfer mixture to small bowl of an electric mixer. Beat in eggs, one at a time, beating until the mixture is thick and glossy before adding the next egg.

4 Drop rounded teaspoons of mixture about 4cm apart on lightly greased oven trays. Bake in moderately hot oven about 15 minutes or until choux pastry is puffed. Reduce oven temperature to moderate; bake 10 minutes or until browned and crisp.

5 Make a small slit in base of choux puffs to allow steam to escape. Return puffs to a moderate oven for about 10 minutes or until dry. Cool to room temperature. Cut a small hole in base of puffs.

6 Just before serving, place the crème pâtissière in a piping bag fitted with a 1cm plain tube; fill the puffs with crème pâtissière. Serve drizzled with chocolate liqueur sauce.

crème pâtissière Bring milk and vanilla bean to a boil in medium saucepan; remove from heat, stand 10 minutes. Remove vanilla bean. Whisk egg yolks and sugar in large bowl until thick and creamy. Whisk in the sifted flour then gradually whisk in the milk. Return mixture to saucepan; cook over low heat, whisking constantly, until mixture boils and thickens. Simmer, whisking constantly, for 2 minutes. Remove from heat, transfer to medium bowl. Cover the surface with plastic wrap; refrigerate until cold.

chocolate liqueur sauce Combine chocolate, butter and cream in small saucepan; stir over low heat until chocolate is melted. Stir in liqueur.

serves 6

per serving 37.5g fat; 2734kJ (654 cal)
tips The unfilled choux puffs are suitable to freeze.
If the choux puffs have softened, re-crisp for a few minutes in a moderate oven; cool before filling.

poached pears with chocolate cream   FRANCE

PREPARATION TIME **15 MINUTES**   COOKING TIME **15 MINUTES**

The pears can be poached a day ahead. The chocolate cream is best made close to serving.

4 medium ripe pears (920g), peeled, halved, cored
1 litre (4 cups) water
1 cinnamon stick
1 vanilla bean, halved lengthways
½ cup (110g) sugar
200g dark eating chocolate, chopped
½ cup (125ml) cream

1 Combine pears, the water, cinnamon, vanilla and sugar in medium saucepan; stir over medium heat until sugar is dissolved. Bring to a boil; simmer, covered, about 8 minutes or until pears are just tender, drain.

2 Meanwhile, combine chocolate and cream in small saucepan; stir over low heat about 5 minutes or until smooth.

3 Pour chocolate cream over pears to serve; add a scoop of vanilla ice-cream, if desired.

serves 4

per serving 25.9g fat; 2345kJ (561 cal)
tip Canned pears could be substituted for fresh pears to save time.

deep-dish apple pie

USA

PREPARATION TIME 45 MINUTES (plus refrigeration time)
COOKING TIME 50 MINUTES (plus cooling time)

1 cup (150g) plain flour
½ cup (75g) self-raising flour
¼ cup (35g) cornflour
¼ cup (30g) custard powder
1 tablespoon caster sugar
100g cold butter, chopped
1 egg, separated
⅓ cup (80ml) cold water, approximately
1 tablespoon caster sugar, extra

FILLING
10 medium granny smith apples (1.5kg)
½ cup (125ml) water
¼ cup (55g) sugar
1 teaspoon grated lemon rind
¼ teaspoon ground cinnamon

1 Sift flours, custard powder and sugar into large bowl, rub in butter (or process flours, custard powder, sugar and butter until mixture resembles breadcrumbs). Add egg yolk and enough water to make ingredients cling together (or process until ingredients just come together). Press dough into a ball, knead on floured surface until smooth; refrigerate 30 minutes.

2 Preheat oven to hot. Divide dough into two portions. Roll one portion between sheets of baking paper until large enough to line base and side of deep 25cm pie plate. Lift pastry into pie plate. Spoon filling into pastry case, brush edge with egg white.

3 Roll remaining pastry until large enough to cover filling. Press edges together; trim edge. Brush pastry with egg white. Decorate with pastry scraps, if desired; brush with a little more egg white, sprinkle with extra sugar. Bake in hot oven 20 minutes; reduce heat to moderate, bake 25 minutes or until pastry is browned.

filling Peel, quarter, core and slice apples. Combine apples in large saucepan with the water, cover; simmer about 5 minutes or until apples are tender. Drain apples, discard liquid. Transfer apples to large bowl; stir in sugar, rind and cinnamon, cool.

serves 8

per serving 11.5g fat; 1417kJ (339 cal)
tip The pie can be made a day ahead; store, covered, in the refrigerator.

lemon tart FRANCE

PREPARATION TIME 20 MINUTES (plus refrigeration time) COOKING TIME 1 HOUR 10 MINUTES (plus cooling time)

1¼ cups (185g) plain flour
⅓ cup (55g) icing sugar mixture
¼ cup (30g) almond meal
125g cold butter, chopped
1 egg yolk

LEMON FILLING
1 tablespoon finely grated lemon rind
½ cup (125ml) lemon juice
5 eggs
¾ cup (165g) caster sugar
300ml thickened cream

1 Blend or process flour, icing sugar, almond meal and butter until combined. Add egg yolk; process until ingredients just come together. Knead dough on floured surface until smooth. Cover; refrigerate 30 minutes.

2 Preheat oven to moderately hot. Grease 24cm-round loose-base flan tin.

3 Roll pastry between sheets of baking paper until large enough to line prepared tin. Ease pastry into tin; trim edges. Cover; refrigerate 30 minutes.

4 Cover pastry with baking paper, fill with dried beans or rice; place tin on oven tray. Bake in moderately hot oven 10 minutes. Remove paper and beans; bake about 10 minutes or until tart shell browns lightly. Remove from oven; reduce oven temperature to moderately slow. Refrigerate cooled pastry case until cold.

5 Pour lemon filling into pastry case. Bake, uncovered, in moderately slow oven about 40 minutes or until filling just sets. Stand 10 minutes; refrigerate lemon tart until cold.

lemon filling Whisk ingredients in medium bowl. Stand 5 minutes; strain.

serves 8

per serving 33.2g fat; 2149kJ (514 cal)

tip Uncooked rice or dried beans used to weigh down the pastry are not suitable for eating. Use them every time you bake-blind; store in an airtight storage jar.

pecan pie   USA

PREPARATION TIME **25 MINUTES (plus refrigeration time)**   COOKING TIME **55 MINUTES (plus cooling time)**

1¼ cups (185g) plain flour
⅓ cup (55g) icing sugar mixture
125g cold butter, chopped
1 egg yolk
1 teaspoon lemon juice, approximately
2 cups (200g) whole pecans
6 egg yolks, extra
½ cup (175g) golden syrup
½ cup (100g) firmly packed
   brown sugar
90g butter, melted, extra
¼ cup (60ml) cream

1 Combine flour and icing sugar in medium bowl; rub in butter. Add egg yolk and enough juice to make ingredients cling together. Knead gently on a floured surface until smooth; wrap in plastic wrap, refrigerate 30 minutes.

2 Roll pastry between sheets of baking paper until large enough to line the base and side of a 24cm-round loose-based flan tin. Peel off top piece of baking paper; lift and invert pastry into tin; press into side then peel off paper.

3 Gently smooth pastry over base and side of tin to avoid air pockets. Trim pastry by running the blade of a sharp knife along edge or by pressing rolling pin over top of flan tin. Cover; refrigerate for 1 hour.

4 Preheat oven to moderate. Cover pastry with baking paper and fill with dried beans or rice. Place flan tin on oven tray; bake in moderate oven for 15 minutes. Remove paper and beans; bake pastry case 5 minutes or until browned lightly.

5 Place pecans on oven tray; bake in moderate oven for 5 minutes or until fragrant. Place nuts in pastry case. Combine extra egg yolks, syrup, brown sugar, extra butter and cream in large bowl; whisk until smooth. Pour mixture over pecans; bake in moderate oven about 30 minutes or until set, cool. Serve with cream, if desired.

serves 8

per serving 50g fat; 2788kJ (667 cal)
tips The uncooked pastry can be stored (wrapped securely in plastic) in the refrigerator for two days or frozen for up to two months.
Uncooked rice or dried beans used to weigh down the pastry are not suitable for eating. Use them every time you bake-blind; store in an airtight storage jar.

peach clafouti   FRANCE

PREPARATION TIME **15 MINUTES**   COOKING TIME **50 MINUTES**

This simple dessert consists of a pancake batter poured over fruit and baked. Any type of canned or stewed fruit can be used.

3 medium peaches (450g), sliced thinly
⅓ cup (50g) plain flour
2 tablespoons self-raising flour
¼ cup (55g) caster sugar
3 eggs, beaten lightly
2 cups (500ml) milk
1 teaspoon vanilla essence

1 Grease shallow 1.5-litre (6 cup) ovenproof dish, place peaches in dish. Preheat oven to moderate.

2 Combine sifted flours and sugar in bowl, gradually stir in egg, then milk and essence; mix to a smooth batter or blend or process mixture.

3 Pour batter into dish over the back of a spoon. Bake in moderate oven for about 50 minutes or until a knife inserted in centre comes out clean. Serve warm with cream or ice-cream.

serves 6

per serving   6.3g fat; 805kJ (192 cal)

tiramisu ITALY

PREPARATION TIME 25 MINUTES (plus cooling and refrigeration time)

1¼ cups (310ml) boiling water
1½ tablespoons dry instant coffee
1 cup (250ml) marsala
250g packet savoiardi sponge
   finger biscuits
½ cup (125ml) thickened cream
¼ cup (40g) icing sugar mixture
2 cups (500g) mascarpone cheese
40g dark eating chocolate, grated

1 Combine the water and coffee in small bowl; stir until dissolved. Stir in ⅔ cup (160ml) of the marsala; cool.

2 Dip half of the biscuits in coffee mixture. Place biscuits in single layer over base of deep 2.5-litre (10 cup) glass dish.

3 Beat cream and sifted icing sugar in small bowl until soft peaks form; transfer to large bowl. Fold in mascarpone and remaining marsala.

4 Spread half the cream mixture over biscuits in dish. Dip remaining biscuits in coffee mixture; place over cream layer. Top biscuits with remaining cream mixture; sprinkle with chocolate. Cover; refrigerate several hours or overnight.

serves 6

per serving 39.2g fat; 2952kJ (705 cal)
tip This recipe is best made a day ahead; store, covered, in the refrigerator.

steamed christmas pudding   ENGLAND

PREPARATION TIME 25 MINUTES   COOKING TIME 5 HOURS 15 MINUTES (plus cooling time)

3¼ cups (500g) mixed fruit, chopped
¾ cup (125g) chopped dried
  seedless dates
¾ cup (125g) chopped raisins
1 cup (250ml) water
1 cup (200g) firmly packed brown sugar
125g butter
1 teaspoon bicarbonate of soda
2 eggs, lightly beaten
1 cup (150g) plain flour
1 cup (150g) self-raising flour
1 teaspoon mixed spice
½ teaspoon ground cinnamon
2 tablespoons dark rum

1 Combine fruit, the water, sugar and butter in saucepan. Stir constantly over heat until butter is melted and sugar dissolved; bring to a boil. Reduce heat; simmer, uncovered, 8 minutes, stir in soda. Transfer mixture to large bowl, stir in eggs, sifted dry ingredients and rum.

2 Grease 2.5-litre (10 cup) pudding steamer. Spoon pudding mixture into prepared steamer. Top with pleated baking paper (to allow for expansion of pudding as it cooks) and foil; secure with string or lid. Place pudding in large boiler with enough boiling water to come halfway up side of steamer. Cover boiler with tight-fitting lid; boil 5 hours. Replenish with boiling water as required. Stand pudding 15 minutes before turning onto a plate; cool.

3 Wrap pudding in plastic wrap, return to clean steamer, or seal tightly in freezer bag or airtight container; refrigerate or freeze.

4 To reheat pudding, remove pudding from plastic wrap and return to steamer. Steam 2 hours following cooking instructions in step 2.

serves 10

per serving 12.3g fat; 2073kJ (496 cal)
tip The pudding can also be reheated in the microwave oven; reheat 4 single serves at a time.

lemon meringue pie   USA

PREPARATION TIME 30 MINUTES (plus refrigeration and standing time)   COOKING TIME 30 MINUTES (plus cooling time)

1½ cups (225g) plain flour
1 tablespoon icing sugar mixture
140g cold butter, chopped
1 egg yolk, beaten lightly
2 tablespoons cold water,
    approximately

FILLING
½ cup (75g) cornflour
1 cup (220g) caster sugar
½ cup (125ml) lemon juice
1¼ cups (310ml) water
2 teaspoons grated lemon rind
3 egg yolks
60g unsalted butter

MERINGUE
3 egg whites
½ cup (110g) caster sugar

1 Sift flour and icing sugar into bowl, rub in butter. Add egg yolk and enough water to make ingredients cling together. Press dough into ball, knead gently on floured surface until smooth; cover, refrigerate 30 minutes.

2 Preheat oven to moderately hot. Roll dough on floured surface until large enough to line 24cm-round loose-base flan tin. Lift pastry into tin, ease into side; trim edge.

3 Place tin on oven tray, line pastry with paper, fill with dried beans or rice. Bake in moderately hot oven 10 minutes. Remove paper and beans; bake 10 minutes or until pastry is lightly browned, cool.

4 Reduce oven temperature to moderate. Spread filling into pastry case, top with meringue. Bake in moderate oven 5 minutes or until meringue is lightly browned. Stand 5 minutes before serving.

filling Combine cornflour and sugar in medium saucepan, gradually stir in juice and the water; stir until smooth. Stir over heat until mixture boils and thickens (mixture should be very thick). Reduce heat; simmer, stirring, 30 seconds. Remove from heat, quickly stir in rind, yolks and butter, stir until butter is melted; cover, cool to room temperature.

meringue Beat egg whites in small bowl with electric mixer until soft peaks form; gradually add sugar, beating until dissolved after additions.

serves 6

per serving 31.8g fat; 2909kJ (696 cal)
tips This recipe can be made a day ahead; store, covered, in the refrigerator.
Uncooked rice or dried beans used to weigh down the pastry are not suitable for eating.
Use them every time you bake-blind; store in an airtight storage jar.

baking

Some of the world's best-known and most-loved recipes are for
baked goods – cakes, muffins, cookies and biscuits, tortes and friands.
Made up of a range of treats, from countries as diverse as America,
France, Portugal and Scotland, this is a collection of the classics.

blueberry muffins   USA

PREPARATION TIME **10 MINUTES**   COOKING TIME **20 MINUTES**

2 cups (300g) self-raising flour
¾ cup (150g) firmly packed
**   brown sugar**
1 cup (150g) fresh or
**   frozen blueberries**
1 egg, beaten lightly
¾ cup (180ml) buttermilk
½ cup (125ml) vegetable oil

1 Preheat oven to moderately hot. Grease
10 holes of a 12-hole (⅓ cup/80ml)
muffin pan.

2 Sift dry ingredients into large bowl,
stir in remaining ingredients.

3 Spoon mixture into prepared holes. Bake in
moderately hot oven about 20 minutes.

makes 10

per muffin 8g fat; 745kJ (178 cal)

chocolate chip cookies USA

PREPARATION TIME 20 MINUTES COOKING TIME 12 MINUTES (plus cooling time)

One story suggests that these were created by a housewife in Massachusetts, in the United States, in 1929. They are also known as toll house cookies.

90g butter
1 teaspoon vanilla essence
⅓ cup (75g) caster sugar
⅓ cup (75g) firmly packed brown sugar
1 egg
½ cup (75g) self-raising flour
¾ cup (105g) plain flour
¾ cup (135g) choc bits
½ cup (50g) chopped pecans
 or walnuts
1 tablespoon milk

1 Preheat oven to moderate. Beat butter, essence and sugars in small bowl with electric mixer until light and fluffy; beat in egg. Stir in flours, choc bits, nuts and milk.

2 Drop heaped tablespoons of mixture, about 3cm apart, onto lightly greased oven trays.

3 Bake in moderate oven about 12 minutes or until firm and lightly browned. Stand on trays 5 minutes before lifting onto wire racks to cool.

makes 18

per cookie 8.7g fat; 690kJ (165 cal)
tip These cookies can be made four days ahead and stored in an airtight container; they are also suitable to freeze.

christmas cake

ENGLAND

PREPARATION TIME **40 MINUTES**
COOKING TIME **3 HOURS 30 MINUTES** (plus cooling time)

3 cups (500g) sultanas
1½ cups (250g) raisins, chopped
⅔ cup (140g) red glacé cherries, quartered
¾ cup (125g) dried currants
¾ cup (125g) mixed peel
2 tablespoons marmalade
½ cup (125ml) rum
250g butter, softened
1 teaspoon grated orange rind
1 teaspoon grated lemon rind
1 cup (200g) firmly packed brown sugar
4 eggs
2 cups (300g) plain flour
2 teaspoons mixed spice
1 cup (160g) blanched almonds, approximately
2 tablespoons rum, extra

1 Preheat oven to slow. Line base and sides of deep 19cm-square or deep 22cm-round cake pan with three thicknesses of baking paper, bringing paper 5cm above edge of pan.

2 Mix fruit, marmalade and rum in large bowl.

3 Beat butter, rinds and sugar in small bowl with electric mixer until just combined; beat in eggs, one at a time, until just combined between additions.

4 Stir butter mixture into fruit mixture; mix in sifted flour and spice. Spread mixture into prepared pan, decorate with blanched almonds.

5 Bake in slow oven 3½ hours. Brush extra rum over top, cover hot cake, in pan, with foil; cool.

serves 16

per serving 20.3g fat; 2245kJ (537 cal)
tip This Christmas cake can be made 3 months ahead and stored, covered, in the refrigerator; it is also suitable to freeze.

palmiers FRANCE

PREPARATION TIME **15 MINUTES (plus refrigeration time)** COOKING TIME **20 MINUTES (plus cooling time)**

These traditional Parisian specialties are named after a palm tree because, when baked, they resemble palm fronds. Palmiers were probably invented as a way to make use of puff pastry scraps; quick and easy, they're great for afternoon tea.

375g packet frozen puff pastry, thawed
2 tablespoons caster sugar, approximately

1 Roll pastry on surface sprinkled with sugar into 20cm x 35cm rectangle; trim edges with sharp knife. Sprinkle pastry lightly with a little more sugar. Fold in long sides of rectangle so that they meet in the centre, sprinkle with a little more sugar, fold in half lengthways, press lightly; cover, refrigerate 30 minutes.

2 Preheat oven to moderately hot. Cut pastry roll into 12mm slices; place slices about 10cm apart on lightly greased oven trays.

3 Bake in moderately hot oven 10 minutes. Turn palmiers with eggslice; bake about 10 minutes or until crisp. Lift onto wire racks to cool. Lightly dust with sifted icing sugar, if desired.

makes 25

per palmier 3.6g fat; 251kJ (60 cal)
serving suggestions Palmiers can be drizzled with melted dark or white chocolate or a thin icing. Drizzle the melted chocolate or the icing over hot palmiers, so that it sets upon cooling.
tip Palmiers can be made two days ahead and stored in an airtight container; they are also suitable to freeze when uncooked.

panforte ITALY

PREPARATION TIME **15 MINUTES**   COOKING TIME **55 MINUTES (plus cooling time)**

Rice paper is a fine, edible paper that is very useful in the making of biscuits, such as macaroons. Contrary to popular belief, it is not actually made from rice but from the pith of a small tree which grows in Asia. Rice paper can be found in specialist food stores and some delicatessens.

2 sheets rice paper
¾ cup (110g) plain flour
2 tablespoons cocoa powder
½ teaspoon ground cinnamon
½ teaspoon ground ginger
½ cup (150g) coarsely chopped glacé figs
½ cup (85g) seedless dried dates, halved
½ cup (125g) coarsely chopped
  glacé peaches
¼ cup (50g) red glacé cherries, halved
¼ cup (50g) green glacé cherries, halved
½ cup (80g) blanched almonds, toasted
½ cup (75g) unsalted cashews, toasted
½ cup (75g) hazelnuts, toasted
½ cup (75g) macadamia nuts, toasted
⅓ cup (115g) honey
⅓ cup (75g) caster sugar
⅓ cup (75g) firmly packed brown sugar
2 tablespoons water
100g dark eating chocolate, melted

1 Preheat oven to moderately slow.

2 Grease 20cm sandwich pan; line base with rice paper sheets.

3 Sift flour, cocoa and spices into large bowl; stir in fruit and nuts. Combine honey, sugars and the water in small saucepan; stir over heat, without boiling, until sugar dissolves. Simmer; uncovered, without stirring, 5 minutes. Pour hot syrup then chocolate into nut mixture; stir until well combined. Press mixture firmly into prepared pan. Bake in moderately slow oven about 45 minutes; cool in pan.

4 Remove panforte from pan; wrap in foil. Stand overnight; cut into thin wedges to serve.

makes 30 wedges

per wedge 7.4g fat; 631kJ (151 cal)

black forest cake

GERMANY

PREPARATION TIME **35 MINUTES**
COOKING TIME **1 HOUR 50 MINUTES (plus cooling time)**

250g butter
1 tablespoon instant coffee powder
1½ cups (375ml) hot water
200g dark eating chocolate, chopped
2 cups (440g) caster sugar
1½ cups (225g) self-raising flour
1 cup (150g) plain flour
¼ cup (25g) cocoa powder
2 eggs
2 teaspoons vanilla essence
600ml thickened cream
¼ cup (60ml) kirsch
2 x 425g cans cherries, drained, halved

1 Preheat oven to slow. Grease deep 23cm-round cake pan, line base and side with baking paper; grease paper well.

2 Melt butter in medium saucepan, stir in combined coffee and hot water, then chocolate and sugar; stir over low heat, without boiling, until smooth. Transfer to large bowl, cool to warm. Beat mixture on low speed with electric mixer; gradually beat in sifted dry ingredients, in three batches. Beat in eggs, one at a time, then essence. Pour into prepared pan. Bake in slow oven about 1¾ hours. Stand 5 minutes before turning onto wire rack to cool.

3 Beat cream until firm peaks form. Trim top of cake to make it flat. Split cake into three even layers. Place one layer onto serving plate, brush with one-third of the kirsch, top with one-third of the cream and half of the cherries. Repeat layering once more, then top with cake-top. Brush top of cake with remaining kirsch; spread with remaining cream.

serves 12

per serving 15.8g fat; 1115kJ (267 cal)
serving suggestion Decorate the top of the cake with fresh cherries and chocolate curls, if desired.
tip Black forest cake will keep for up to three days if stored, covered, in the refrigerator.

portuguese custard tarts   PORTUGAL

PREPARATION TIME **25 MINUTES (plus thawing time)**   COOKING TIME **30 MINUTES (plus cooling time)**

3 egg yolks
½ cup (110g) caster sugar
2 tablespoons cornflour
¾ cup (180ml) cream
½ cup (125ml) water
strip of lemon rind
2 teaspoons vanilla essence
1 sheet ready-rolled butter puff pastry

1 Preheat oven to hot.

2 Grease 12-hole (⅓ cup/80ml) muffin pan. Place egg yolks, sugar and cornflour in medium saucepan and whisk them until combined. Gradually whisk in cream and the water until smooth.

3 Add lemon rind; stir over medium heat until mixture just comes to a boil. Remove from heat immediately; remove rind and stir in essence.

4 Cut pastry sheet in half. Remove the plastic and stack the two halves on top of each other. Stand about 5 minutes or until thawed. Roll the pastry up tightly from the short side then cut the log into 12 x 1cm rounds.

5 Lay pastry on lightly floured board and roll each round out to about 10cm. Press rounds into prepared muffin pan with your fingers. Spoon custard into pastry cases.

6 Bake tarts in hot oven about 20 minutes or until well browned. Transfer to a wire rack to cool.

makes 12

per tart 10.1g fat; 677kJ (162 cal)

tip These custard tarts are best made on the day of serving.

scones   SCOTLAND

PREPARATION TIME 15 MINUTES   COOKING TIME 15 MINUTES

2 cups (300g) self-raising flour
2 teaspoons sugar
15g butter, chopped coarsely
1 cup (250ml) milk
½ cup (160g) strawberry jam
½ cup (125ml) thickened
**   cream, whipped**

1 Place flour and sugar in medium bowl; rub in butter. Make well in centre of flour mixture; add most of the milk. Using a knife, "cut" milk through flour mixture to mix to soft, sticky dough. Add remaining milk only if mixture is too dry. Preheat oven to very hot.

2 Turn dough from bowl onto lightly floured surface; knead dough lightly until smooth. Press dough out gently and evenly until approximately 2cm thick. Using cutter, cut 5cm rounds from dough. Gently knead remaining dough into round shape, press dough out; cut 5cm rounds from dough. Place scones, side by side and just touching, in lightly greased 20cm sandwich pan. Brush tops of rounds with a little extra milk.

3 Bake scones in very hot oven about 15 minutes or until tops are browned.

4 Serve warm scones with jam and cream.

makes 10

per scone 7.2g fat; 911kJ (218 cal)

chilli corn bread

USA

PREPARATION TIME 20 MINUTES
COOKING TIME 1 HOUR (plus cooling time)

1 cup (150g) self-raising flour
1 teaspoon salt
1 cup (170g) cornmeal
½ cup (100g) kibbled rye
1 tablespoon brown sugar
1 teaspoon ground cumin
2 tablespoons chopped fresh flat-leaf parsley
1 teaspoon chopped fresh thyme
½ cup (60g) grated cheddar cheese
310g can creamed corn
⅔ cup (90g) frozen corn kernels, thawed
⅔ cup (160ml) buttermilk
⅓ cup (80ml) milk
2 teaspoons sambal oelek
2 eggs, beaten lightly
50g butter, melted

1 Preheat oven to moderately hot. Grease deep
   19cm-square cake pan; line base with baking paper.

2 Sift flour and salt into large bowl, stir in cornmeal,
   rye, sugar, cumin, herbs and cheese.

3 Combine remaining ingredients in medium bowl;
   mix well, stir into dry ingredients.

4 Spread mixture into prepared pan, bake in moderately
   hot oven about 1 hour. Stand, covered, 10 minutes
   before turning onto wire rack to cool.

serves 10

per serving 9.1g fat; 1100kJ (263 cal)

chocolate brownies USA

PREPARATION TIME 25 MINUTES COOKING TIME 55 MINUTES (plus cooling time)

An American creation, brownies are extravagantly rich and luscious, and usually made with lashings of chocolate.

30g butter
250g dark eating chocolate, chopped finely
80g butter, extra
2 teaspoons vanilla essence
1 cup (200g) firmly packed brown sugar
2 eggs
½ cup (75g) plain flour
½ cup (75g) chopped roasted hazelnuts
⅓ cup (80g) sour cream

CHOCOLATE ICING
125g dark eating chocolate, chopped
60g butter

1 Preheat oven to moderate. Grease deep 19cm-square cake pan, line base with baking paper; grease paper.

2 Melt butter in medium saucepan, add chocolate, stir over low heat until chocolate is melted; cool 5 minutes.

3 Beat extra butter, essence and sugar in small bowl with electric mixer until light and fluffy; beat in eggs one at a time. Transfer mixture to large bowl. Stir in sifted flour, then chocolate mixture, nuts and cream.

4 Spread mixture into prepared pan. Bake in moderate oven about 45 minutes; cool in pan.

5 Turn slice from pan, remove paper. Spread slice with chocolate icing; cut when set.

chocolate icing Melt chocolate and butter in small bowl over saucepan of simmering water; cool to room temperature. Beat with wooden spoon until thick and spreadable.

makes 12

per brownie 28.1g fat; 1778kJ (425 cal)
tip Brownies can be made three days ahead and stored in an airtight container; they are also suitable to freeze.

shortbread SCOTLAND

PREPARATION TIME **15 MINUTES** COOKING TIME **30 MINUTES** (plus cooling time)

Originally a hogmanay (New Year's Eve) specialty of Scotland, where it originated up to 400 years ago, shortbread has become very popular in many parts of the globe and is now eaten any time of year.

250g butter, at room
    temperature
⅓ cup (75g) caster sugar
2 cups (300g) plain flour
½ cup (75g) rice flour or
    ground rice

1 Preheat oven to slow. Beat butter and sugar in small bowl with electric mixer until combined. Add large spoonfuls of sifted flours to butter mixture, beating after each addition.

2 Press ingredients together gently, knead on floured surface until smooth.

3 Divide dough into two portions; shape portions into 18cm rounds. Place rounds on greased oven trays; mark each round into 12 wedges, prick with fork. Pinch a decorative edge with floured fingers.

4 Bake in slow oven about 30 minutes. Stand 10 minutes before transferring to wire rack to cool. Cut when cold.

makes 24 wedges

per wedge 8.7g fat; 598kJ (143 cal)
tip Shortbread can be made a month ahead and stored in an airtight container; it is also suitable to freeze.

fruit mince pies

ENGLAND

PREPARATION TIME 45 MINUTES
(plus refrigeration and standing time)
COOKING TIME 20 MINUTES

No traditional Christmas feast would be complete without a batch of these delicious festive treats. Fruit mince is available in jars or you can make your own using the recipe below.

2 cups (300g) plain flour
2 tablespoons almond meal
180g cold butter, chopped
1 teaspoon grated lemon rind
¼ cup (40g) icing sugar mixture
1 egg yolk
¼ cup (60ml) milk, approximately
1 egg, beaten lightly
icing sugar mixture

FRUIT MINCE
1 small apple (130g), peeled, cored
½ cup (80g) sultanas
⅓ cup (55g) mixed peel
2 tablespoons glacé cherries, chopped
⅓ cup (50g) currants
⅓ cup (55g) blanched whole
    almonds, chopped
1 cup (200g) firmly packed
    brown sugar
½ teaspoon grated lemon rind
1 tablespoon lemon juice
½ teaspoon grated orange rind
½ teaspoon ground cinnamon
½ teaspoon mixed spice
¼ teaspoon ground nutmeg
40g butter, melted
2 tablespoons brandy

1 Lightly grease two 12-hole shallow patty pans.

2 Sift flour into bowl, stir in almond meal, rub in butter. Stir in rind and sifted icing sugar. Stir in yolk and enough milk to make ingredients cling together. Knead dough on floured surface until smooth, cover; refrigerate 30 minutes.

3 Preheat oven to moderately hot. Roll pastry until 3mm thick. Cut out 7.5cm rounds, place in patty pans. Drop tablespoons of fruit mince into each pastry case.

4 Roll scraps of pastry on floured surface, cut out desired shapes. Brush each pastry shape with egg, place egg-side down on fruit mince.

5 Bake in moderately hot oven about 20 minutes or until lightly browned. Dust with a little sifted icing sugar before serving.

fruit mince Finely chop apple and half of the sultanas; combine in bowl with remaining sultanas and remaining ingredients, mix well. Transfer mixture to sterilised jar. Store in refrigerator for at least 3 days before using. Makes about 2 cups (500g) fruit mince.

makes 24

per pie 10.6g fat; 1058kJ (253 cal)
tip These pies can be made a week ahead and stored in an airtight container; they are also suitable to freeze for up to two months.

mississippi mud cake   USA

PREPARATION TIME **10 MINUTES**   COOKING TIME **1 HOUR 30 MINUTES** (plus standing and cooling time)

250g butter, chopped
150g dark eating chocolate, chopped
2 cups (440g) sugar
1 cup (250ml) hot water
⅓ cup (80ml) whisky
1 tablespoon instant coffee powder
1½ cups (225g) plain flour
¼ cup (35g) self-raising flour
¼ cup (25g) cocoa powder
2 eggs, beaten lightly

1   Preheat oven to moderately slow. Grease 23cm-square slab pan, line base with baking paper; grease paper.

2   Combine butter, chocolate, sugar, the water, whisky and coffee in medium saucepan; stir over low heat until chocolate is melted and mixture is smooth, cool to lukewarm.

3   Stir in sifted flours and cocoa, then egg. Pour into prepared pan. Bake in moderately slow oven about 1¼ hours. Stand 10 minutes before turning onto wire rack to cool. Serve dusted with sifted icing sugar, if desired.

serves 12

per serving   14.2g fat; 1240kJ (297 cal)
serving suggestion   Serve this dense, moist cake with whipped cream and fresh raspberries, if desired.
tip   Mississippi mud cake will keep for up to five days; store, covered, in the refrigerator.

anzac biscuits   AUSTRALIA

PREPARATION TIME **20 MINUTES**   COOKING TIME **25 MINUTES** (plus cooling time)

It is thought that Anzac biscuits were not named until after the first World War, when they were made and sold as fundraisers for returned soldiers. It is best to use traditional (not quick-cook) oats in our version.

1 cup (90g) rolled oats
1 cup (150g) plain flour
1 cup (220g) sugar
¾ cup (60g) desiccated coconut
125g butter
1 tablespoon golden syrup
1 teaspoon bicarbonate of soda
2 tablespoons boiling water

1 Preheat oven to slow. Combine oats, sifted flour, sugar and coconut in large bowl.

2 Combine butter and golden syrup in medium saucepan; stir over low heat until butter is melted. Combine soda and the water, add to butter mixture; stir into dry ingredients while mixture is warm.

3 Place 3-level-teaspoon portions of mixture, about 4cm apart, on greased oven trays; press down lightly.

4 Bake in slow oven about 20 minutes or until golden brown. Loosen biscuits while warm, cool on trays.

makes 30

per biscuit 5g fat; 426kJ (102 cal)
tip Anzac biscuits can be made four days ahead and stored in an airtight container; they are also suitable to freeze.

genoise sponge

FRANCE

PREPARATION TIME **35 MINUTES (plus refrigeration time)**
COOKING TIME **30 MINUTES (plus cooling time)**

This is a light-textured sponge; the mixture is beaten over
hot water to give volume and extra lightness. It is correct that
plain flour is used. Melted butter should be cooled to room
temperature before being added.

4 eggs
½ cup (110g) caster sugar
⅔ cup (100g) plain flour
60g butter, melted
300ml thickened cream
1 tablespoon icing sugar mixture
¼ cup (80g) strawberry jam, warmed
500g strawberries, sliced thinly
1 tablespoon icing sugar mixture, extra

1 Preheat oven to moderate. Grease deep 20cm-round cake pan,
line base with baking paper; grease paper. Combine eggs and
sugar in large heatproof bowl, place over saucepan of simmering
water. Do not allow water to touch base of bowl. Using a rotary
beater or electric mixer, beat until mixture is thick and creamy,
about 10 minutes. Remove bowl from saucepan; beat mixture
until it returns to room temperature.

2 Sift half of the flour over egg mixture, carefully fold in flour;
fold in remaining sifted flour.

3 Quickly and carefully fold in cooled melted butter. Pour mixture
into prepared pan, bake in moderate oven about 20 minutes
or until sponge feels elastic to touch. Turn immediately onto
wire rack to cool.

4 Beat cream and icing sugar in small bowl with electric mixer until
soft peaks form. Split sponge in half; place one half, cut-side up,
on serving plate. Spread with jam and cream; top with strawberries,
then remaining sponge half.

5 Decorate cake with extra sifted icing sugar and strawberries,
if desired.

serves 8

per serving 23g fat; 1572kJ (376 cal)
tip This cake can be frozen, unfilled, for up to one month.

lamingtons AUSTRALIA

PREPARATION TIME 1 HOUR COOKING TIME 30 MINUTES (plus cooling time)

The cake is easier to handle if it's a little stale; day-old cake is ideal. Sponge or butter cake can also be used. Fill lamingtons with jam and cream, if desired.

6 eggs
⅔ cup (150g) caster sugar
⅓ cup (50g) cornflour
½ cup (75g) plain flour
⅓ cup (50g) self-raising flour
2 cups (180g) desiccated coconut,
  approximately

ICING
4 cups (500g) icing sugar mixture
½ cup (50g) cocoa powder
15g butter, melted
⅔ cup (160ml) milk

1 Preheat oven to moderate. Grease 23cm-square slab pan. Beat eggs in medium bowl with electric mixer about 10 minutes or until thick and creamy. Gradually beat in sugar, until dissolved after each addition. Fold in triple-sifted flours.

2 Spread mixture into prepared pan; bake in moderate oven about 30 minutes. Turn cake onto wire rack to cool.

3 Cut cake into 16 squares, dip squares in icing; drain off excess icing, toss squares in coconut. Place lamingtons on wire rack to set.

icing Sift icing sugar and cocoa into heatproof bowl; stir in butter and milk. Stir icing over pan of simmering water until it is of a coating consistency.

makes 16

per lamington 11.4g fat; 1350kJ (323 cal)

florentines

ITALY

PREPARATION TIME 25 MINUTES   COOKING TIME 10 MINUTES (plus cooling time)

¾ **cup (120g) sultanas**
2 cups (60g) corn flakes
¾ **cup (105g) roasted peanuts, chopped**
½ **cup (125g) chopped red glacé cherries**
⅔ **cup (160ml) sweetened condensed milk**
150g dark eating chocolate, melted

1   Preheat oven to moderate. Combine sultanas, corn flakes, peanuts, cherries and milk in bowl; mix well.

2   Place 1½-tablespoon portions of mixture about 5cm apart on baking-paper-lined oven trays.

3   Bake in moderate oven about 10 minutes or until lightly browned; cool on trays.

4   Spread base of each biscuit with chocolate. Make wavy lines in chocolate with fork just before chocolate sets.

makes 18

per florentine 6.3g fat; 686kJ (164 cal)

tips Florentines can be made a month ahead and stored, covered, in the refrigerator; they are also suitable to freeze.

To melt chocolate, choose a heatproof bowl that just fits inside a small saucepan; add enough water to pan to come almost to the level of the bottom of the bowl, then bring water to a boil. Chop chocolate roughly, and place in bowl over the pan of boiling water. Remove pan from heat, and stir constantly until chocolate is melted.

sacher torte

AUSTRIA

PREPARATION TIME 30 MINUTES (plus standing time)
COOKING TIME 40 MINUTES (plus cooling time)

There are countless variations of the traditionally secret recipe for
this cake. This is our favourite version.

150g dark eating chocolate, chopped
1 tablespoon water
150g butter
½ cup (110g) caster sugar
3 eggs, separated
1 cup (150g) plain flour
2 tablespoons caster sugar, extra
1 cup (320g) apricot jam

CHOCOLATE ICING
125g dark eating chocolate, chopped
125g butter

1 Preheat oven to moderate. Grease deep 23cm-round
cake pan, line base with baking paper; grease paper.

2 Melt chocolate in heatproof bowl over hot water. Stir in
the water; cool to room temperature.

3 Cream butter and sugar in small bowl with electric mixer until light
and fluffy. Beat in egg yolks one at a time, beat until combined.
Transfer mixture to large bowl, stir in chocolate mixture, then sifted
flour. Beat egg whites in small bowl until soft peaks form, gradually
add extra sugar, beat until dissolved between each addition; fold
lightly into chocolate mixture. Spread into prepared pan. Bake in
moderate oven about 30 minutes. Stand 5 minutes before turning
onto wire rack to cool; leave cake upside down.

4 Split cold cake in half; place one half, cut-side up, on serving
plate. Heat and strain jam; brush half of the jam over cake half.
Top with remaining cake half, brush cake all over with remaining
jam. Stand about 1 hour at room temperature to allow jam to set.
Spread top and side of cake with icing, set at room temperature.

chocolate icing Melt chocolate and butter in bowl over
hot water, stir until smooth. Cool at room temperature until
spreadable, stirring occasionally; this can take up to 2 hours.
This icing is also suitable for piping.

serves 10

per serving 32.3g fat; 2317kJ (553 cal)
tip Sacher torte will keep for two days; store, covered,
in the refrigerator.

almond and strawberry friands

FRANCE

PREPARATION TIME **10 MINUTES**
COOKING TIME **25 MINUTES (plus cooling time)**

Friand pans are available from specialty cookware and kitchen stores. Muffin pans can also be used.

185g butter, melted
1 cup (125g) almond meal
6 egg whites, beaten lightly
1½ cups (240g) icing sugar mixture
½ cup (75g) plain flour
100g strawberries, sliced thinly

1 Preheat oven to moderately hot.

2 Grease 12-hole (⅓ cup/80ml) friand pan.

3 Combine butter, almond meal, egg whites, sugar and flour in medium bowl; stir until just combined. Divide mixture among prepared holes; scatter with strawberry slices.

4 Bake in moderately hot oven about 25 minutes; stand in pan 5 minutes, turn onto wire rack to cool.

5 Serve dusted with a little extra sifted icing sugar, if desired.

makes 12

per friand 18.5g fat; 1175kJ (281 cal)

menus
from around the world

greek easter lunch
Tzatziki p23
Taramasalata p22
Dolmades p21
Spanakopita p12
Roasted lamb with
 lemon potatoes p72
Tomato, olive and fetta salad p145

italian feast
Marinated vegetables p14
Asparagus risotto p131
Veal parmigiana p61
Rocket and parmesan salad p140
Cassata p182

warming french dinner
French onion soup p40
Coq au vin p120
Poached pears with
 chocolate cream p201

tex-mex fiesta
Guacamole p10
Chilli con carne p49
Beef burritos p48
Chilli corn bread p222

simple japanese dinner
Tuna sashimi p24
Teriyaki beef p54
Vegetable tempura p134

friday-night italian
Frittata with onions and zucchini p171
Pizza p175
Lemon gelato p184

spanish summer lunch
Gazpacho p29
Potato tortilla p169
Paella p106

middle-eastern buffet
Hummus p11
Baba ghanoush p17
Felafel p16
Lamb kofta p70
Chicken tagine with
 dates and honey p122
Almond coriander couscous p159
Fattoush p138
Tabbouleh p146

hearty italian meal
Osso buco p53
Soft polenta p164
Tiramisu p207

long, lazy french lunch
Chicken liver and port pâté p25
Quiche lorraine p170
Salade niçoise p151
Peach clafouti p206

australia-day feast
Beef, tomato and pea pies p56
Pavlova 190
Anzac biscuits p229

casual thai lunch
Tom yum goong p34
Fish cakes p92
Pad thai p84
Spicy beef salad p144

special thai dinner
Tom ka gai p30
Massaman beef curry p50
Chicken larb p143

american cafe lunch
Crab cakes p103
Meatloaf with caramelised onion p57
Coleslaw p153
Lemon meringue pie p209

chinese banquet
Crab and prawn wontons p18
Sang choy bow p82
Spicy pork ribs p80
Honey prawns p90
Salt and pepper squid p93
Stir-fried asian greens p156
Combination fried rice p168

fast vietnamese dinner
Fresh rice paper rolls with prawns p19
Pho p32
Chicken and cabbage salad p142

english sunday lunch
Pea and ham soup p35
Roast beef with
 yorkshire puddings p46
Lemon delicious p188

italian seafood dinner
Spaghetti alla vongole p94
Fish milanese p97
Tomato and bocconcini salad p147
Panna cotta p192

indian dinner party
Samosas with coriander yogurt p20
Rogan josh p76
Pork vindaloo p88
Chicken tikka p113
Mixed dhal p124
Cucumber and mint raita p157

glossary

allspice also known as pimento or jamaican pepper; available whole or ground. Tastes like a blend of cinnamon, clove and nutmeg.

almonds flat, pointy-ended nuts with pitted brown shell enclosing brown skin, underneath which lies a creamy white kernel.

blanched brown skins removed.

meal also known as ground almonds; nuts are powdered to a coarse flour texture, for use in baking or as a thickening agent.

slivered small lengthways-cut pieces.

flaked paper-thin slices.

anise also known as aniseed or sweet cumin, the seeds are the fruit of an annual plant native to Greece and Egypt. Dried, they have a strong licorice flavour. Whole and ground seeds are available.

arrowroot a starch made from the rhizome of a Central American plant; used mostly for thickening. Cornflour can be substituted but will not give as clear a glaze.

bacon rashers also known as slices of bacon; made from pork side, cured and smoked. Streaky bacon is the fatty end of a bacon rasher (slice) without the lean (eye) meat.

baking powder a raising agent consisting mainly of two parts cream of tartar to one part bicarbonate of soda (baking soda). The acid and alkaline combination, when moistened and heated, gives off carbon dioxide which aerates and lightens the mixture during baking.

bamboo shoots the creamy-yellow young shoots of bamboo plants, available fresh and in cans.

barbecue sauce a spicy, tomato-based sauce used to marinate or baste, or as a condiment.

basil an aromatic herb which has both culinary and medicinal uses. There are many types of basil, and the appearance of the leaves and the scent varies, but the most commonly used basil in cooking is sweet basil.

sweet basil also known as common basil; has strong smell similar to cloves or licorice. Available in most greengrocers and supermarkets; use the leaves only.

thai basil also known as bai kaprow, thai basil has slightly smaller leaves and a strong, somewhat bitter, flavour.

bay leaves aromatic leaves from the bay tree; usually purchased dried.

bean sprouts also known as bean shoots; tender new growths of assorted beans and seeds germinated for consumption. The most readily available are mung bean, soy bean, alfalfa and snow pea sprouts.

beer beverage brewed from malted barley and other cereals, yeast and water, and flavoured with hops. Usually contains 5% alcohol or lower.

beetroot also known as red beets; firm, round root vegetable.

bicarbonate of soda also known as baking soda.

bok choy also known as bak choy, pak choi, chinese white cabbage or chinese chard; has a mild mustard taste. Use stems and leaves. Baby bok choy is smaller and more tender than bok choy and often cooked whole.

brandy spirit distilled from wine.

breadcrumbs

packaged fine-textured, crunchy, purchased, white breadcrumbs.

stale one- or two-day-old bread made into crumbs by grating, blending or processing.

broad beans also known as fava beans; available fresh, canned and frozen. Fresh are best peeled twice (discarding both the outer long green pod and the sandy-green tough inner shell).

burghul also known as bulghur wheat; hulled, steamed wheat kernels that, once dried, are crushed into various-sized grains. Used in Middle-Eastern dishes such as kibbeh and tabbouleh.

butter use salted or unsalted (sweet) butter; 125g is equal to one stick of butter.

buttermilk sold alongside fresh milk in supermarkets; despite the implication of its name, is low in fat. Originally the liquid left after cream was separated from milk, today, it is commercially made similarly to yogurt.

capers the grey-green buds of a warm climate (usually Mediterranean) shrub, sold either dried and salted or pickled in a vinegar brine; used to enhance sauces and dressings with their piquant flavour.

capsicum also known as bell pepper or, simply, pepper. Native to Central and South America, they can be red, green, yellow, orange or purplish-black. Seeds and membranes should be discarded before use.

caraway seeds a member of the parsley family; available in seed or ground form.

cardamom can be purchased in pod, seed or ground form. Has a distinctive aromatic, sweetly rich flavour and is one of the world's most expensive spices.

cayenne pepper a thin-fleshed, long, extremely-hot red chilli; purchased dried and ground.

cellophane noodles also known as bean thread noodles, bean thread vermicelli or glass noodles; should be soaked in boiling water to soften. They can also be deep-fried.

cheese

blue mould-treated cheeses mottled with blue veining. Varieties include firm and crumbly Stilton types to mild, creamy brie-like cheeses.

bocconcini from the diminutive of boccone, meaning mouthful, is the term used for a delicate, semi-soft, white cheese traditionally made in Italy from buffalo milk. Spoils rapidly so must be kept under refrigeration, in brine, for one or two days at most.

cheddar the most widely eaten cheese in the world, cheddar is a semi-hard cow-milk cheese originally made in England. It ranges in colour from white to pale yellow and has a slightly crumbly texture if properly matured. It's aged for between nine months and two years, and the flavour becomes sharper with time.

fetta a white cheese with milky, fresh acidity, fetta is one of the cornerstones of the Greek, Turkish and Bulgarian kitchens. It is most commonly made from cow milk, though sheep- and goat-milk varieties are available. Fetta is sometimes described as a pickled cheese because it is matured in brine for at least a month; this imparts a strong salty flavour. Fetta is solid but crumbles readily.

gruyère a Swiss cheese having small holes and a nutty, slightly salty flavour.

mascarpone a cultured cream product made in much the same way as yogurt. It's whitish to creamy yellow in colour, with a soft, creamy texture, a fat content of 75% and a slightly tangy taste.

mozzarella a soft, spun-curd cheese. It has a low melting point and wonderfully elastic texture when heated, and is used to add texture rather than flavour.

parmesan also known as parmigiano, parmesan is a hard, grainy cow-milk cheese. The curd is salted in brine for a month before being aged for up to two years.

pecorino generic Italian name for cheeses made from sheep milk. It's a hard, white to pale yellow cheese, traditionally made from November to June when the sheep are grazing on natural pastures. Pecorino is usually matured for eight to 12 months and is known for the region in which it's produced.

ricotta the name for this soft, white, cow-milk cheese roughly translates as cooked again. It's made from whey, a byproduct of other cheese making, to which fresh milk and acid are added. Ricotta is a sweet, moist cheese with a fat content of around 8.5% and a slightly grainy texture.

romano this hard sheep-milk cheese has been made in the countryside around Rome since the 1st century AD. Widely exported since that time because of its excellent keeping qualities, romano is now made in other parts of the world from cow milk. Straw-coloured and grainy in texture, it's mainly used for grating. Parmesan can be substituted.

chickpeas also called garbanzos, hummus or channa; an irregularly round, sandy-coloured legume.

chillies available in many different types and sizes. Use rubber gloves when seeding and chopping fresh chillies as they can burn your skin. Removing seeds and membranes lessens the heat level.

dutch medium-hot but flavoursome, fairly long fresh chilli; sometimes referred to as a holland chilli.

dried flakes crushed dried chillies.

jalapeño fairly hot green chillies. Sold finely chopped or whole, bottled in vinegar, as well as fresh; we used the medium-hot, sweetish chopped bottled version in our recipes.

powder the Asian variety is the hottest, made from ground chillies; it can be used as a substitute for fresh chillies in the proportion of teaspoon ground chilli powder to 1 medium chopped fresh chilli.

thai small, hot chillies, bright-red to dark-green in colour.

chinese cabbage also known as peking or napa cabbage, wong bok and petsai, the pale green, crinkly leaves of this elongated cabbage only require brief cooking.

chives related to the onion and leek; possess subtle onion flavour. Chives and flowering chives are interchangeable.

choc bits also known as chocolate chips and chocolate morsels; available in milk, white and dark chocolate. Made of cocoa liquor, cocoa butter, sugar and an emulsifier, these hold their shape in baking and are ideal for decorating.

chocolate, dark we used eating chocolate; made of cocoa liquor, cocoa butter and sugar.

chorizo a sausage of Spanish origin, made of coarsely ground pork and highly seasoned with garlic and chillies.

choy sum also known as flowering bok choy, flowering white cabbage or chinese flowering cabbage; the stems, leaves and yellow flowers are served steamed, stir-fried and in soups.

ciabatta in Italian, the word means slipper, which is the traditional shape of this popular white bread with a crisp crust.

clams we used a ridge-shelled variety of this bivalve mollusc; also known as vongole.

clove dried flower buds of a tropical tree; can be used whole or in ground form.

coconut

cream the first pressing from grated mature coconut flesh; available in cans and cartons.

desiccated unsweetened, concentrated, dried finely shredded coconut.

milk the second pressing (less rich) from grated mature coconut flesh; available in cans and cartons.

coriander also known as cilantro or chinese parsley; bright-green leafy herb with a pungent flavour.

corn flakes crisp flakes of corn.

cornflour also known as cornstarch; used as a thickening agent in cooking.

cornmeal often called polenta, to which this ground corn (maize) is similar, albeit coarser. One can be substituted for the other, but textures will vary.

couscous a fine, grain-like cereal product, originally from North Africa; made from semolina.

cream we used fresh cream in this book, unless otherwise stated, also known as pure cream and pouring cream; has no additives unlike commercially thickened cream. Minimum fat content is 35%.

crème fraîche mature fermented cream having a slightly tangy, nutty flavour and velvety texture. Used in savoury and sweet dishes. Minimum fat content is 35%.

sour a thick commercially cultured soured cream good for dips, toppings and baked cheesecakes. Minimum fat content is 35%.

thickened a whipping cream containing a thickener. Minimum fat content is 35%.

crunchy fried noodles crispy egg noodles packaged (commonly a 100g packet) already deep-fried and sometimes labelled as crunchy noodles.

cumin ground spice also known as zeera.

currants dried, tiny, almost-black raisins so-named after a grape variety that originated in Corinth, Greece.

curry leaves available fresh or dried and possessing a mild curry flavour; use like bay leaves.

custard powder instant mixture used to make pouring custard; similar to North American instant pudding mixes.

daikon a basic food in Japan; also known as giant white radish.

dashi a basic fish and seaweed stock used in many Japanese dishes; made from dried bonito flakes and kelp. Instant dashi powder, also known as dashi-no-moto, is a concentrated granulated powder. Available from Asian specialty stores.

eggs some recipes in this book call for raw or barely cooked eggs; exercise caution if there is a salmonella problem in your area.

eggplant also known as aubergine.

eschalots also called french shallots, golden shallots or shallots; small, elongated, brown-skinned members of the onion family. Grow in tight clusters similar to garlic.

essence extract.

evaporated milk unsweetened canned milk from which water is extracted by evaporation.

fennel also known as finocchio or anise; also the name given to dried seeds having a licorice flavour.

fish sauce also called nam pla or nuoc nam; made from pulverised salted fermented fish, most often anchovies. Has a pungent smell and strong taste; use sparingly.

flour

plain an all-purpose flour, made from wheat.

rice a very fine flour, made from ground white rice, flour milled from rye.

self-raising plain flour sifted with baking powder in the proportion of 1 cup flour to 2 teaspoons baking powder.

wholemeal self-raising also known as wholewheat flour; has raising agent added.

galangal resembles ginger but is dense, fibrous and harder to cut than ginger. Available in Asian specialty stores.

garam masala a blend of spices based on cardamom, cinnamon, cloves, coriander, fennel and cumin, roasted and ground together. Black pepper and chilli can be added for a hotter version.

gelatine we used powdered gelatine; also available in sheets, known as leaf gelatine.

gelatinous noodles (shirataki) also called devil's tongue noodles; thin, translucent and jelly-like, they have a crunchy texture, but little flavour, and are available fresh or dried. Keep fresh noodles in the refrigerator.

ghee clarified butter; with the milk solids removed, this fat can be heated to a high temperature without burning.

glacé fruit fruit that has been preserved in sugar syrup.

golden syrup a byproduct of refined sugarcane; pure maple syrup or honey can be substituted.

grand marnier orange-flavoured liqueur based on Cognac-brandy.

horseradish cream a prepared paste of grated horseradish, vinegar, oil and sugar.

jam also known as preserve or conserve; most often made from fruit.

kaffir lime leaves dried leaves used as flavourings; substitute strips of fresh lemon or lime rind.

kecap manis Indonesian thick soy sauce which has sugar and spices added.

kirsch cherry-flavoured liqueur.

kumara Polynesian name of orange-fleshed sweet potato often confused with yam.

lamb noisettes a loin chop with the bone removed and the "tail" wrapped around the meaty centre.

lamb shanks, french-trimmed also known as drumsticks or frenched shanks; the gristle and narrow end of the bone is discarded then the remaining meat trimmed.

lamington pan a straight-sided rectangular slab cake pan that is 3cm deep.

lebanese cucumber long, slender and thin-skinned; this variety also known as the european or burpless cucumber.

leek a member of the onion family, resembles the green onion but is much larger.

lemon grass a tall, clumping, lemon-smelling and -tasting, sharp-edged grass; the white lower part of each stem is chopped and used in Asian cooking.

lentils dried pulses often identified by and named after their colour (red, brown, yellow).

lotus root is available in cans, or dried form, which needs soaking in hot water with a dash of lemon juice for about 20 minutes. Fresh lotus root is occasionally available.

maple syrup a thin syrup distilled from the sap of the maple tree. Maple-flavoured syrup or pancake syrup is not an adequate substitute for the real thing.

marmalade a preserve, usually based on citrus fruit.

mesclun is a salad mix or gourmet salad mix with a mixture of assorted young lettuce and other green leaves, including baby spinach leaves, mizuna, curly endive.

mince meat also known as ground meat, as in beef, pork, lamb, chicken and veal.

mirin a Japanese champagne-coloured cooking wine; made of glutinous rice and alcohol and used expressly for cooking. Should not be confused with sake; there is a seasoned sweet mirin called manjo mirin that is made of water, rice, corn syrup and alcohol.

mixed peel candied citrus peel.

mixed spice a blend of ground spices usually consisting of cinnamon, allspice and nutmeg.

mushroom

button small, cultivated white mushrooms with a mild flavour.

shiitake also known as donko or chinese mushrooms, have a unique meaty flavour popular in the Asian kitchen. Often sold dried; soak to rehydrate before use.

mustard

dijon a pale brown, distinctively flavoured fairly mild French mustard.

powder finely ground white (yellow) mustard seeds.

seeds the black seeds are also known as brown mustard seeds; more pungent than the white (or yellow) seeds used in most prepared mustards.

wholegrain also known as seeded. A French-style coarse-grain mustard made from crushed mustard seeds and dijon-style French mustard.

nutmeg the dried nut of an evergreen tree native to Indonesia; it is available in ground form or you can grate your own with a fine grater.

oak leaf lettuce also known as feville de chene; available in both red and green leaf.

oil

olive made from ripened olives. Extra virgin and virgin are the best, while extra light or light refers to taste, not fat levels.

peanut pressed from ground peanuts; most commonly used oil in Asian cooking because of its high smoke point.

sesame made from roasted, crushed white sesame seeds. Do not use for frying.

vegetable any of a number of oils sourced from plants rather than animal fats.

onion

green also known as scallion or (incorrectly) shallot; an immature onion picked before the bulb has formed, having a long, bright-green edible stalk.

red also known as spanish, red spanish or bermuda onion; a sweet-flavoured, large, purple-red onion.

spring onions with small white bulbs, long green leaves and narrow green-leafed tops.

oyster sauce Asian in origin, this rich, brown sauce is made from oysters and their brine, cooked with salt and soy sauce, and thickened with starches.

paprika ground dried red capsicum (bell pepper), available sweet or hot.

parsley, flat-leaf also known as continental or italian parsley.

peanut butter peanuts ground to a paste; available in crunchy and smooth varieties.

pearl barley barley that has had its outer husk (bran) removed, and been steamed and polished before being used in cooking.

pecans native to the United States; golden-brown, buttery and rich nut.

pickled ginger, pink (gari) available, packaged, from Asian grocery stores; pickled paper-thin shavings of ginger in a mixture of vinegar, sugar and natural colouring.

pitta also known as Lebanese bread. This wheat-flour pocket bread is sold in large, flat pieces that separate into two thin rounds. Also available in small thick pieces called pocket pitta.

plum sauce a thick, sweet and sour dipping sauce made from plums, vinegar, sugar, chillies and spices.

polenta a flour-like cereal made of ground corn (maize); similar to cornmeal but finer and lighter in colour; also the name of the dish made from it.

prawns also known as shrimp.

puff pastry, frozen packaged frozen puff pastry, available from supermarkets.

quiche pastry, frozen ready-rolled packaged sheets of frozen puff pastry, especially suitable for quiches, available from supermarkets.

purslane a small plant with reddish stems and rounded leaves with a mild flavour and crisp texture; can be eaten raw or cooked.

raisins dried sweet grapes.

rice noodle sheets made from rice flour and water, available from Asian specialty stores.

rice paper contrary to popular belief, rice paper isn't made from rice but from the pith of a small tree which grows in Asia. The fine, glossy paper is edible and is very useful in the making of biscuits, such as macaroons. In China and Japan, where the tree is widely cultivated, rice paper is used to make artificial flowers. This variety, generally imported from Holland, is whiter than the other and looks more like a grainy sheet of paper. It is used in confectionery making and baking, and not eaten uncooked.

rice paper rounds softened in hot water, used as a wrapper for fresh vegetables, prawns, etc., to make an uncooked spring roll; generally served at room temperature. Made from ground rice flour, salt and water; imported from South-East Asia and sold packaged in either round or square pieces.

rice

arborio small round-grain rice; well suited to absorb a large amount of liquid, especially good in risottos.

medium-grain previously sold as calrose rice; extremely versatile rice that can be substituted for short- or long-grain rices if necessary.

short-grain fat, almost round grain with a high starch content; tends to clump together when cooked.

rigani, dried wild oregano, native to Greece; an integral part of a traditional Greek salad. Replace with dried oregano if unavailable.

rocket also known as arugula, rugula and rucola; a peppery-tasting green leaf which can be eaten raw in salad or used in cooking. Baby rocket leaves are both smaller and less peppery.

rum, dark we prefer to use an underproof rum (not overproof) for a more subtle flavour.

saffron stigma of a member of the crocus family, available in strands or ground form; imparts a yellow-orange colour to food once infused. Quality varies greatly; should be stored in the freezer.

sake Japan's favourite rice wine; is used in cooking, marinating and as part of dipping sauces. If sake is unavailable, dry sherry, vermouth or brandy can be used as a substitute.

sambal oelek (also ulek or olek) Indonesian in origin; a salty paste made from chillies, garlic and ginger.

savoiardi sponge finger biscuits also known as savoy biscuits, lady's fingers or sponge fingers, they are Italian-style crisp fingers made from sponge-cake mixture.

savoy cabbage large, heavy head with crinkled dark-green outer leaves; a fairly mild tasting cabbage.

semolina made from durum wheat; milled various-textured granules, all of these finer than flour.

sherry dry fortified wine consumed as an aperitif or used in cooking. Sold as fino (light, dry), amontillado (medium sweet, dark) and oloroso (full-bodied, very dark).

shrimp paste also known as trasi and blanchan; a strong-scented, almost solid preserved paste that is made of salted dried shrimp. This pungent flavouring is used in many South-East Asian soups and sauces.

sichuan peppercorns also known as chinese pepper. Small, red-brown aromatic seeds resembling black peppercorns; they have a peppery-lemon flavour.

silverbeet also known as swiss chard and mistakenly called spinach; a member of the beet family grown for its tasty green leaves and celery-like stems. Best cooked rather than eaten raw.

soy made from fermented soy beans. Several variations are available in most supermarkets and Asian food stores.

spinach also known as english spinach and incorrectly, silverbeet. Tender green leaves are good uncooked in salads or added to soups, stir-fries and stews just before serving.

split peas also known as field peas; green or yellow pulse grown especially for drying, split in half along a centre seam. Used in soups, stews and, occasionally, spiced and cooked on their own.

star anise a dried star-shaped fruit of a tree native to China. The pods have an astringent aniseed flavour – widely used in the Asian kitchen. Available whole and ground, it is an essential ingredient in five-spice powder.

stock available in cans or cartons. Stock cubes or powder can be used. As a guide, 1 teaspoon of stock powder or 1 small crumbled stock cube mixed with 1 cup (250ml) water will give a fairly strong stock. Be aware of the salt and fat content of stock cubes and powders and prepared stocks. To make your own stock, see recipes on page 246.

sugar we used coarse, granulated table sugar, also known as crystal sugar, unless otherwise specified.

brown an extremely soft, fine granulated sugar retaining molasses for its characteristic colour and flavour.

caster also known as superfine or finely granulated table sugar.

icing mixture also known as confectioners' sugar or powdered sugar; granulated sugar crushed together with a small amount (about 3%) of cornflour added.

icing pure also known as confectioners' sugar or powdered sugar.

palm also known as jaggery, jawa melaka and gula melaka; from the coconut palm. Dark-brown to black in colour and usually sold in rock-hard cakes, the sugar of choice in Indian and most South-East Asian cooking. Palm sugar can be substituted with brown or black sugar.

sultanas dried grapes, also known as golden raisins.

sweetened condensed milk milk from which 60% of the water has been removed; the remaining milk is then sweetened with sugar.

tabasco sauce brand name of an extremely fiery sauce made from vinegar, hot red peppers and salt.

taco seasoning mix a packaged seasoning meant to duplicate the Mexican sauce made from oregano, cumin, chillies and other spices.

tahini a rich, sesame-seed paste, used in most Middle-Eastern cuisines.

tamarind concentrate a thick, purple-black, ready-to-use paste extracted from the pulp of the tamarind bean; stirred into sauces and casseroles to add a sour flavour.

tarama salted, dried roe of grey mullet fish.

toasted seaweed sheets a type of dried seaweed used in Japanese cooking. Sold in thin sheets.

tofu also known as bean curd, an off-white, custard-like product made from the "milk" of crushed soy beans; comes fresh as soft or firm, and processed as fried or pressed dried sheets.

tomato

canned whole peeled tomatoes in natural juices.

egg also called plum or roma, these are smallish, oval-shaped tomatoes.

juice available in cans, bottles and cartons from supermarkets.

paste triple-concentrated tomato puree used to flavour soups, stews and sauces.

sauce also known as ketchup or catsup; a flavoured condiment made from tomatoes, vinegar and spices.

tortillas thin, round, unleavened bread originating in Mexico; can be made at home or purchased frozen, fresh or vacuum-packed. Two kinds are available, one made from wheat flour and the other from corn.

turmeric a member of the ginger family, its root is dried and ground, resulting in the rich yellow powder that gives many Indian dishes their characteristic colour. It is intensely pungent in taste but not hot.

vanilla bean dried long, thin pod from a tropical orchid grown in Central and South America and Tahiti; the minuscule black seeds inside the bean are used to impart a luscious vanilla flavour.

vine leaves we used vine leaves in brine; available in jars and packets.

vinegar

balsamic authentic only from the province of Modena, Italy; made from a regional wine of white Trebbiano grapes processed then aged in antique wooden casks to give the exquisite pungent flavour.

brown malt made from fermented malt and beech shavings.

cider made from fermented apples.

red wine based on fermented red wine.

rice a colourless vinegar made from fermented rice and flavoured with sugar and salt. Also known as seasoned rice vinegar.

rice wine made from rice wine lees (sediment), salt and alcohol.

sherry natural vinegar aged in oak according to the traditional Spanish system; mellow wine vinegar named for its colour.

white made from spirit of cane sugar.

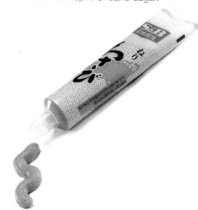

wasabi an Asian horseradish used to make the pungent, green-coloured sauce served with Japanese raw fish dishes; sold in powdered or paste form.

water chestnuts resemble chestnuts in appearance; small brown tubers with crisp, white, nutty-tasting flesh. Best experienced fresh, however, canned water chestnuts are more easily obtained and can be kept about a month, once opened, under refrigeration.

whisky we used a good quality Scotch whisky.

wine we used good-quality dry white and red wines in our recipes.

wonton wrappers gow gee, egg or spring roll pastry sheets can be substituted. The wrappers are made of flour, eggs and water; purchase in the refrigerator cases of Asian markets. Store in the refrigerator or freezer; bring to room temperature before using.

worcestershire sauce a thin, dark-brown spicy sauce used as a seasoning for meat, gravies and cocktails, and as a condiment.

yeast a 7g (¼ oz) sachet of dried yeast (2 teaspoons) is equal to 15g (½ oz) compressed yeast if substituting one for the other.

yogurt plain, unflavoured yogurt, in addition to being good eaten on its own, can be used as a meat tenderiser, as the basis for various sauces and dips or as an enricher and thickener.

zucchini also known as courgette. Green, yellow or grey; a member of the squash family having edible flowers.

index

make your own stock

These recipes can be made up to 4 days ahead and kept, covered, in the refrigerator. Remove any fat from the surface after the cooled stock has been refrigerated overnight. If stock is to be kept longer, divide it into smaller quantities then freeze it. All the recipes below make approximately 2.5 litres (10 cups) of stock.

Stock is also available in cans or cartons; stock cubes or powder can also be used. As a guide, 1 teaspoon of stock powder or 1 small crumbled stock cube mixed with 1 cup (250ml) water will result in a fairly strong stock. Be aware of the salt and fat content of these products.

beef stock

2kg meaty beef bones
2 medium onions (300g)
2 sticks celery, chopped
2 medium carrots (250g), chopped
3 bay leaves
2 teaspoons black peppercorns
5 litres (20 cups) water
3 litres (12 cups) water, extra

Place bones and unpeeled chopped onions in baking dish. Bake in hot oven about 1 hour or until well browned. Transfer bones and onions to large saucepan; add celery, carrots, bay leaves, peppercorns and the water. Simmer, uncovered, 3 hours. Add extra water; simmer, uncovered, 1 hour. Strain.

chicken stock

2kg chicken bones
2 medium onions (300g), chopped
2 sticks celery, chopped
2 medium carrots (250g), chopped
3 bay leaves
2 teaspoons black peppercorns
5 litres (20 cups) water

Combine ingredients in large saucepan; simmer, uncovered, 2 hours. Strain.

fish stock

1.5kg fish bones
3 litres (12 cups) water
1 medium onion (150g), chopped
2 sticks celery, chopped
2 bay leaves
1 teaspoon black peppercorns

Combine ingredients in large saucepan; simmer, uncovered, 20 minutes. Strain.

vegetable stock

2 large carrots (360g), chopped
2 large parsnips (360g), chopped
4 medium onions (600g), chopped
12 sticks celery, chopped
4 bay leaves
2 teaspoons black peppercorns
6 litres (24 cups) water

Combine ingredients in large saucepan; simmer, uncovered, 1½ hours. Strain.

facts & figures

Wherever you live, you'll be able to use our recipes with the help of these easy-to-follow conversions. While these conversions are approximate only, the difference between an exact and the approximate conversion of various liquid and dry measures is but minimal and will not affect your cooking results.

dry measures

metric	imperial
15g	1/2oz
30g	1oz
60g	2oz
90g	3oz
125g	4oz (1/4lb)
155g	5oz
185g	6oz
220g	7oz
250g	8oz (1/2lb)
280g	9oz
315g	10oz
345g	11oz
375g	12oz (3/4lb)
410g	13oz
440g	14oz
470g	15oz
500g	16oz (1lb)
750g	24oz (11/2lb)
1kg	32oz (2lb)

liquid measures

metric	imperial
30ml	1 fluid oz
60ml	2 fluid oz
100ml	3 fluid oz
125ml	4 fluid oz
150ml	5 fluid oz (1/4 pint/1 gill)
190ml	6 fluid oz
250ml	8 fluid oz
300ml	10 fluid oz (1/2 pint)
500ml	16 fluid oz
600ml	20 fluid oz (1 pint)
1000ml (1 litre)	13/4 pints

helpful measures

metric	imperial
3mm	1/8in
6mm	1/4in
1cm	1/2in
2cm	3/4in
2.5cm	1in
5cm	2in
6cm	21/2in
8cm	3in
10cm	4in
13cm	5in
15cm	6in
18cm	7in
20cm	8in
23cm	9in
25cm	10in
28cm	11in
30cm	12in (1ft)

measuring equipment

The difference between one country's measuring cups and another's is, at most, within a 2 or 3 teaspoon variance. (For the record, one Australian metric measuring cup holds approximately 250ml.) The most accurate way of measuring dry ingredients is to weigh them. When measuring liquids, use a clear glass or plastic jug with the metric markings. (One Australian metric tablespoon holds 20ml; one Australian metric teaspoon holds 5ml.)

Note: North America, NZ and the UK use 15ml tablespoons. All cup and spoon measurements are level.

We use large eggs having an average weight of 60g.

how to measure

When using graduated metric measuring cups, shake dry ingredients loosely into the appropriate cup. Do not tap the cup on a bench or tightly pack the ingredients unless directed to do so. Level top of measuring cups and measuring spoons with a knife. When measuring liquids, place a clear glass or plastic jug with metric markings on a flat surface to check accuracy at eye level.

oven temperatures

These oven temperatures are only a guide. Always check the manufacturer's manual.

	°C (Celsius)	°F (Fahrenheit)	Gas Mark
Very slow	120	250	1
Slow	150	300	2
Moderately slow	160	325	3
Moderate	180 – 190	350 – 375	4
Moderately hot	200 – 210	400 – 425	5
Hot	220 – 230	450 – 475	6
Very hot	240 – 250	500 – 525	7

Senior editor *Julie Collard*
Designer *Caryl Wiggins*
Food editor *Louise Patniotis*
Special feature photographer *Andre Martin*
Special feature stylist *Kirsty Cassidy*
Special feature home economist *Cathie Lonnie*
Food director *Pamela Clark*
Nutritional information *Amira Ibram*

ACP Books Staff
Editorial director *Susan Tomnay*
Creative director *Hieu Chi Nguyen*
Editorial coordinator *Caroline Lowry*
Editorial assistant *Karen Lai*
Publishing manager (sales) *Brian Cearnes*
Publishing manager (rights & new projects) *Jane Hazell*
Brand manager *Donna Gianniotis*
Pre-press *Harry Palmer*

Production manager *Carol Currie*
Business manager *Sally Lees*
Chief executive officer *John Alexander*
Group publisher *Jill Baker*
Publisher *Sue Wannan*

Produced by ACP books, Sydney.
Printing by Leefung-Asco, China.
Published by ACP Publishing Pty Limited,
54 Park St, Sydney; GPO Box 4088, Sydney, NSW 2001.
Ph: (02) 9282 8618 Fax: (02) 9267 9438.
acpbooks@acp.com.au
www.acpbooks.com.au

To order books phone 136 116.
Send recipe enquiries to
reccipeenquiries@acp.com.au

AUSTRALIA: Distributed by Network Services,
GPO Box 4088, Sydney, NSW 1028.
Ph: (02) 9282 8777 Fax: (02) 9264 3278.
UNITED KINGDOM: Distributed by Australian Consolidated
Press (UK), Moulton Park Business Centre, Red House Rd,
Moulton Park, Northampton, NN3 6AQ.
Ph: (01604) 497 531 Fax: (01604) 497 533
acpukltd@aol.com
CANADA: Distributed by Whitecap Books Ltd,
351 Lynn Ave, North Vancouver, BC, V7J 2C4
Ph: (604) 980 9852 Fax: (604) 980 8197
customerservice@whitecap.ca www.whitecap.ca
NEW ZEALAND: Distributed by Netlink Distribution
Company, ACP Media Centre, Cnr Fanshawe and
Beaumont Streets, Westhaven, Auckland.
PO Box 47906, Ponsonby, Auckland, NZ.
Ph: (9) 366 9966 ask@ndcnz.co.nz

Clark, Pamela
The Australian Women's Weekly Great Cooking Classics
Includes index.
ISBN 1 86396 311 1
1. Cookery. I. Title. II. Title: Great Cooking Classics.
III. Title: Australian Women's Weekly.
641.5

The publishers would like to thank: Bayswiss; Bisanna Tiles;
Bison Homewares Australia; Camargue; Cambodia House;
Country Road Homewares; Design Mode International Pty Ltd;
J.D. Milner & Associates for Le Creuset; Hale Imports Pty Ltd
for Pillivuyt; Mud Australia; and The Art of Food & Wine
for props used in photography.

Photographers: Alan Benson, Scott Cameron, Rob Clark,
Gerry Colley, Brett Danton, Joe Filshie, Rowan Fotheringham,
Louise Lister, Ashley Mackevicius, Andre Martin, Stuart Scott,
Brett Stevens, Rob Taylor, Ian Wallace

Stylists: Myles Beaufort, Wendy Berecry, Janelle Bloom,
Kate Brown, Marie-Helene Clauzon, Amanda Cooper,
Georgina Dolling, Kay Francis, Jane Hann, Trish Heagerty,
Katy Holder, Amber Keller, Cherise Koch, Sarah O'Brien

Cover: Beef, tomato and pea pies, page 56
Photographer: Andre Martin
Stylist: Kirsty Cassidy

Back cover: Genoise sponge, page 230
Photographer: Andre Martin
Stylist: Kirsty Cassidy

greatcookingclassics